The Biological Evidence Preservation Handbook: Best Practices for Evidence Handlers

Technical Working Group on Biological Evidence Preservation

Susan Ballou
Mark Stolorow
Melissa Taylor
Law Enforcement Standards Office
Office of Special Programs

Phylis S. Bamberger
Task Force on Wrongful Convictions
New York State Bar Association

Larry Brown
Los Gatos/Monte Sereno Police Department

Rebecca Brown
Innocence Project

Yvette Burney
Scientific Investigation Division
Los Angeles Police Department

Dennis Davenport
Commerce City Police Department

Lindsay DePalma
Shannan Williams
Booz Allen Hamilton

Cynthia Jones
American University

Ralph Keaton
American Society of Crime Laboratory Directors/
Laboratory Accreditation Board

William Kiley
Joseph Latta
International Association for Property and Evidence

Margaret Kline
Biomolecular Measurement Division
Material Measurements Laboratory

Karen Lanning
Evidence Control Unit
Federal Bureau of Investigation

Gerry LaPorte
Office of Investigative and Forensic Sciences
National Institute of Justice

Linda E. Ledray
Sexual Assault Nurse Examiners/
Sexual Assault Response Team

Randy Nagy
LGC Forensics

Brian E. Ostrom
Portland Metro Forensic Laboratory
Oregon State Police

Lisa Schwind
Office of the Public Defender
State of Delaware

Stephanie Stoiloff
Forensic Services Bureau
Miami-Dade Police Department

http://dx.doi.org/10.6028/NIST.IR.7928

April 2013

U.S. Department of Commerce
Rebecca Blank, Acting Secretary

National Institute of Standards and Technology
Patrick D. Gallagher, Under Secretary of Commerce for Standards and Technology and Director

CONTENTS

FIGURES

TABLES

INTRODUCTION

Across the nation, headlines tell the story of evidence that has been mishandled, misplaced, lost, or destroyed. Often the blame for these mishaps is directed toward property and evidence custodians housed in law enforcement agencies nationwide. Many law enforcement agencies do not properly address, recognize, or support the efforts of their property rooms. Although these agencies bear ultimate responsibility for maintaining the integrity of the evidence, the real problem lies with a systemic failure to properly account for evidence from collection through final disposition. This failure reduces the public's confidence in the criminal justice system to produce just results in criminal and civil proceedings.

Biological evidence refers to samples of biological material—such as hair, tissue, bones, teeth, blood, semen, or other bodily fluids—or to evidence items containing biological material (DNA Initiative 2012). This biological evidence, which may or may not have been previously analyzed at a forensic laboratory, should be retained in an appropriate storage facility until needed for court or for forensic testing. Such evidence is frequently essential in linking someone to or excluding someone from crime scene evidence. The criminal justice system depends on presenting evidence to judges and jurors to help them reach a conclusion about the guilt or innocence of the defendant. All criminal justice stakeholders, including law enforcement officers, lawyers, forensic analysts, and fact finders, should be certain that the biological evidence they are considering has been properly preserved, processed, stored, and tracked to avoid contamination, premature destruction, or degradation. In addition, individuals who come into contact with biological evidence, such as evidence custodians, need to be confident that it has been packaged and labeled in a way that will allow them to efficiently locate relevant evidence for a case. To establish this confidence, all handlers of biological evidence should follow well-defined procedures for its optimal preservation.

The Biological Evidence Preservation Handbook offers guidance for individuals involved in the collection, examination, tracking, packaging, storing, and disposition of biological evidence. This may include crime scene technicians, law enforcement officers, healthcare professionals, forensic scientists, forensic laboratory managers, evidence supervisors, property managers, storage facility personnel, lawyers, testifying experts, court staff members, and anyone else who may come in contact with biological evidence. While many of the recommendations relate to the physical storage, preservation, and tracking of evidence at the storage facility, this handbook also covers the transfer of the material between the storage facility and other locations and discusses how the evidence should be handled at these other locations.

This report is divided into five main sections that detail issues and make recommendations related to biological evidence storage, tracking, preservation, and disposition. A glossary, which provides standard definitions of the technical terms used in this report, follows these sections.

RETAINING BIOLOGICAL EVIDENCE

While most states have established their own statutes and/or policies for biological evidence retention, some have not. It is imperative that high-level guidance be given to biological evidence handlers regarding the circumstances under which evidence must be kept. This section defines recommended best practices for retaining biological evidence, including the length of time such evidence should be kept. It also provides guidance on identifying what biological evidence should be retained.

BIOLOGICAL EVIDENCE HAZARDS AND HANDLING

Contact with bodily fluids can spread disease such as those caused by bloodborne pathogens, and individuals handling biological evidence should treat it as hazardous to ensure safety. This section offers recommendations on various aspects of biological evidence handling, including the use of personal protective equipment (PPE), Federal standards, the management of spills or accidents, and biological waste disposal.

PACKAGING AND STORING BIOLOGICAL EVIDENCE

The use of well-defined procedures for packaging, storing, and tracking can maintain biological evidence integrity for testing. Personnel involved in managing biological evidence often face challenges because of the size and location of the storage facility, supplies available for packaging, adequacy of tracking systems and resources, and other issues. This section identifies current best practices to maintain evidence integrity from initial packaging to final disposition.

CHAIN OF CUSTODY AND EVIDENCE TRACKING

Providing an accurate and complete chain of custody record ensures that the evidence that arrives in court is what was collected at the crime scene. An accurate chain of custody identifies and tracks the evidence from the time it was collected—including the method by which it was obtained—through final disposition for each individual who had possession and responsibility. This section discusses various evidence tracking systems and recommends procedures to improve all aspects of chain-of-custody recordkeeping.

EVIDENCE DISPOSITION

Jurisdictions face limitations because of storage space and preservation requirements and must make choices about when to keep or how to dispose of certain evidence. This section makes recommendations for best practices, policies, and procedures to decide what evidence needs to be retained and the length of time it needs to be retained in accordance with applicable statutes.

TECHNICAL WORKING GROUP ON BIOLOGICAL EVIDENCE PRESERVATION

The recommendations in this document are not mandated by any governing body; they are provided as recommended best practices developed and agreed upon by the Technical Working Group on Biological Evidence Preservation. This working group consists of experts in all aspects of biological evidence preservation (see following list) who have devoted time to researching and documenting the best advice that current technology allows.

The Technical Working Group on Biological Evidence Preservation convened in August 2010 with the goal to provide guidance to evidence custodians who have been traditionally plagued by the lack of such guidance. Little attention has been paid to how handlers of biological evidence should properly store it after collection and through post-conviction. Although storage conditions alone are a major issue, the group quickly discovered that obstacles with biological evidence that need to be addressed to ensure integrity include packaging, proper maintenance and tracking throughout its chain of custody, appropriate disposition, and policies at the state, local, and departmental levels.

Through these analyses and discoveries, the Technical Working Group developed its charge: "To create best practices and guidance to ensure the integrity, prevent the loss, and reduce the premature destruction of biological evidence after collection through post-conviction proceedings."

The working group met nine times over two years. The working group developed this handbook through a consensus process in which each member had an opportunity to influence the recommendations and writing. Despite the diversity of backgrounds and views, the working group was able to reach substantial agreement on most issues, including formal recommendations.

Overall, the document is the working group's best attempt at providing practical guidance while addressing some of the broader issues in evidence management. The storage of biological evidence is just one consideration, albeit a critical one, in a larger system of evidence storage; therefore, the group has put forward some recommendations that can also be applied to other forms of evidence preservation management. The scope of this report, however, is limited to biological evidence only.

The working group hopes that this document is useful in addressing the needs of its readers and will spark an ongoing dialogue about more ways to improve evidence management systems. Please visit http://www.nist.gov/oles/ to obtain more resources to help your organization better preserve its biological evidence.

MEMBERSHIP

Susan Ballou, Program Manager of Forensic Sciences, Law Enforcement Standards Office (OLES), National Institute of Standards and Technology (NIST)

Phylis S. Bamberger, Judge (Retired), Task Force on Wrongful Convictions, New York State Bar Association

Larry Brown, Property Manager, Los Gatos/Monte Sereno Police Department

Rebecca Brown, Director of State Policy Reform, Innocence Project

Yvette Burney, Commanding Officer, Scientific Investigation Division, Los Angeles Police Department

Dennis Davenport, Senior Crime Scene Investigator, Commerce City Police Department

Lindsay DePalma, Contractor, Office of Investigative and Forensic Science, National Institute of Justice (NIJ)

Cynthia Jones, Associate Professor of Law, American University

Ralph Keaton, Executive Director, American Society of Crime Laboratory Directors/Laboratory Accreditation Board

William Kiley, Deputy Police Chief (Retired), Immediate Past President, International Association for Property and Evidence (IAPE)

Margaret Kline, Research Biologist, Biomolecular Measurement Division, NIST

Karen Lanning, Chief, Evidence Control Unit, Federal Bureau of Investigation

Gerry LaPorte, Program Manager, Office of Investigative and Forensic Sciences, NIJ

Joseph Latta, Police Lieutenant (Retired), Executive Director, Lead Instructor, IAPE

Linda E. Ledray, Director, Resource Center, Sexual Assault Nurse Examiners/Sexual Assault Response Team

Randy Nagy, U.S. Market Development Manager, LGC Forensics

Brian E. Ostrom, Criminalist 4, Portland Metro Forensic Laboratory, Oregon State Police

Lisa Schwind, Unit Head, Forensic Service and Education, Office of the Public Defender, State of Delaware

Stephanie Stoiloff, Senior Police Bureau Commander, Forensic Services Bureau, Miami-Dade Police Department

Mark Stolorow, Director, OLES, NIST

STAFF

Shannan Williams, Project Leader, Associate (Booz Allen Hamilton), OLES, NIST

Melissa Taylor, Study Director, OLES, NIST

Jennifer L. Smither, Technical Editor, Science Applications International Corporation

John Swarr, Research Assistant, Booz Allen Hamilton

ACKNOWLEDGEMENTS

The Technical Working Group on Biological Evidence Preservation gratefully acknowledges the following individuals for their contributions to the development and review of this handbook. Reviewers provided constructive suggestions but were not asked to approve or endorse any conclusions or recommendations in the draft handbook. Responsibility for the final content of this handbook rests with the members of the working group.

Kathleen Brown*, Nurse Professor, University of Pennsylvania, School of Nursing

Rockne Harmon, Forensic/Cold Case Consultant, DNARock

Ted Hunt*, Chief Trial Attorney, Jackson County Prosecutor's Office

Jeff Irland, Subject Matter Expert in Automated Identification Technologies (AIT), Booz Allen Hamilton

John Paul Jones*, Working Group Program Manager for Forensic Sciences, OLES, NIST

Dan Katz*, Deputy Director, Maryland State Crime Lab

David Loftis, Managing Attorney, Innocence Project

Anuj Mehta, Subject Matter Expert in AIT, Booz Allen Hamilton

Kenneth Melson, Professional Lecturer in Law, George Washington University Law School

Mitch Morrissey*, District Attorney, Denver Justice Council

Jeffrey Nye*, Biological Program Coordinator, Michigan State Police

Altaf Rahamatulla, Policy Analyst, Innocence Project

Peter Vallone*, Research Chemist, Biomolecular Measurement Division, NIST

* Reviewer

SPONSORSHIP

The NIJ is the research, development, and evaluation agency of the U.S. Department of Justice and is dedicated to researching crime control and justice issues. NIJ provides objective, independent, evidence-based knowledge and tools to meet the challenges of crime and justice. The Office of Investigative and Forensic Sciences is the Federal Government's lead agency for forensic science research and development as well as for the administration of programs that provide direct support to crime laboratories and law enforcement agencies to increase their capacity to process high-volume cases, to provide needed training in new technologies, and to provide support to reduce backlogs. Forensic science program areas include Research and Development in Basic and Applied Forensic Sciences, Coverdell Forensic Science Improvement Grants, DNA Backlog Reduction, Solving Cold Cases with DNA, Post-Conviction DNA Testing Assistance, National Missing and Unidentified Persons System, and Forensic Science Training Development and Delivery.

A non-regulatory agency of the Department of Commerce, the National Institute of Standards and Technology (NIST) promotes U.S. innovation and industrial competitiveness by advancing measurement science, standards, and technology in ways that enhance economic security and improve our quality of life. It accomplishes these actions for the forensic science community through the Law Enforcement Standards Office (OLES) Forensic Science Program, which directs research efforts to develop performance standards, measurement tools, operating procedures, guidelines, and reports that will advance the field of forensic science. OLES also serves the broader public safety community through the promulgation of standards in protective systems; detection, enforcement, and inspection technologies; public safety communication; and counterterrorism and response technologies.

I. RETAINING BIOLOGICAL EVIDENCE

This section provides guidance on preventing the premature destruction of biological evidence. This section focuses on criminal proceedings; however, the retention of biological evidence may be applicable to civil cases and proceedings. This section includes the following:

- guidance regarding biological evidence identification
- recommendations on the retention of biological evidence for certain crime categories
- recommendations on the retention of biological evidence for different case statuses

Preserving and readily retrieving biological evidence from adjudicated and unsolved cases has benefits for all members of the criminal justice system. As the identification power of DNA evidence is recognized, it is clear that crime-solving potential resides latent in biological evidence from crime scenes. Therefore, each state should consider the legal and policy issues that address the retention of biological evidence and should establish procedures that describe the type and length of time for which evidence should be retained for each type of crime. Although most states already have legislation that dictates which categories of crime qualify for long-term storage of biological evidence, some jurisdictions have problems interpreting and implementing policies within property and evidence rooms. For those states and localities in which there is limited or vague guidance or in which stakeholders are reconsidering requirements, the working group recommends the following retention considerations and requirements.

Recommendation I-1:
All persons who have responsibility for the intake and/or storage and disposition of biological evidence should take online, in-classroom, or other forms of training on evidence management.

IDENTIFYING BIOLOGICAL EVIDENCE

Existing state laws vary in their definitions of what constitutes biological evidence in the context of evidence retention. A review of the National Institute of Justice's (2002) list of items from which biological evidence can be found for criminal cases illustrates the variety of items that can be successfully tested with current technology. Further, touch DNA, or DNA contained in shed skin cells that transfer to surfaces that humans touch, can be sampled from countless objects and surfaces (Daly, Murphy, and McDermott 2012).

However, requiring the retention of all physical evidence that can potentially contain DNA would result in the retention of all evidence collected unless it was screened to determine the possible presence of genetic material. Therefore, this handbook's recommendations attempt to balance the interests of justice with practicable storage concerns and to offer a minimum threshold for biological evidence retention. The table below describes different types of evidence that can contain biological evidence, which, in turn could be tested for DNA.

Table I-1: Examples of Sources of Biological Evidence (National Institute of Justice 2002)

Evidence	Likely Location of DNA on the Evidence	Source of DNA
Baseball bat or similar weapon	Handle, end	Sweat, skin, blood, tissue
Hat, bandanna, or mask	Inside	Sweat, hair, dandruff
Eyeglasses	Nose or ear piece, lens	Sweat, skin
Facial tissue, cotton swab	Surface area	Mucus, blood, sweat, semen, ear wax
Dirty laundry	Surface area	Blood, sweat, semen
Toothpick	Tip	Saliva
Used cigarette	Cigarette butt	Saliva
Stamp or envelope	Licked area	Saliva
Tape or ligature	Inside/outside surface	Saliva, skin
Bottle, can, or glass	Side, mouthpiece	Saliva, sweat
Used condom	Inside/outside surface	Semen, vaginal or rectal cells
Blanket, pillow, sheet	Surface area	Sweat, hair, semen, urine, saliva
"Through and through" bullet	Outside surface	Blood, tissue
Bite mark	Person's skin or clothing	Saliva
Fingernail, partial fingernail	Scrapings	Blood, sweat, tissue

Potential sources of biological evidence can include, but are not limited to, the types of evidence listed in Table I-1. In some cases, even these evidence types may not contain DNA or may provide information of no probative value. Therefore, an official with experience, training, and insight into the context of the individual case should ultimately determine if an item could contain biological evidence and should be retained as such. These officials may include detectives, attorneys, investigators, crime scene technicians, and/or crime laboratory staff members. Property and evidence custodians, however, rarely have the expertise or insight into the context of a specific case to make initial determinations of what should be kept and whether it is biological evidence.

Recommendation I-2:
Prior to a property and evidence custodian accepting biological evidence, it should be clearly marked and labeled by the submitter as biological evidence, allowing it to be tracked within the evidence management system and stored appropriately from intake through disposition.

BULKY EVIDENCE: CONSIDERATIONS FOR LONG-TERM EVIDENCE RETENTION

To facilitate forensic testing for trial and post-conviction proceedings, it is essential to store and track as much of the evidence as necessary. However, it may be extremely difficult to maintain large or bulky items of evidence from which biological material is derived. Figure I-1 depicts the collection of biological material from a large bulky item—such as a couch—for forensic testing. For the long term, agencies might find it sufficient to retain samples taken from a large item (see B. and C. in figure I-1) as opposed to the large item on which biological evidence may have been located (see A. in figure I-1). Other examples of bulky evidence include a car, the wall/ceiling of a house, carpet, or another large piece of furniture such as a bed. If the origin of a sample is well documented (such as through photographs or case files), it may not be necessary to store the entire couch for testing and future re-testing.

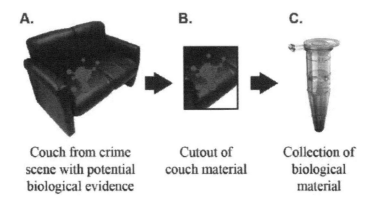

A.	B.	C.
Couch from crime scene with potential biological evidence	Cutout of couch material	Collection of biological material

Figure I-1: Collection of evidence from large/bulky items.

Recommendation I-3:
Property and evidence custodians should consult with investigators, laboratory analysts, and, when appropriate, prosecutors to determine whether only representative sample(s) should be retained in situations in which samples are too large or too costly to store. Property and evidence custodians, investigators, laboratory analysts, and prosecutors should discuss situations in which prosecutors should be consulted. These decisions should not be made exclusively by property and evidence custodians.

RECOMMENDED CRIME CATEGORIES FOR WHICH EVIDENCE SHOULD BE PRESERVED

In addition to defining what should be retained, the category of crimes for which biological evidence should be retained must also be prescribed. Individual state laws vary greatly in this regard (see appendix B for a listing of existing state laws regarding biological evidence retention).

EFFECT OF "CASE STATUS" ON THE RETENTION OF BIOLOGICAL EVIDENCE

When determining the duration of time that biological evidence must be held, it is essential to understand what is meant by "case status" for criminal cases. Generally, there are four categories of case status:

- Open Cases (i.e., no suspect, but investigation continuing)
- Charges Filed (i.e., suspects charged and court proceedings active)
- Adjudicated (i.e., conviction, dismissal, or acquittal)
- Unfounded/Refused/Denied/No Further Investigation

This section provides an overview of each of these categories and discusses the implications of biological evidence disposition for each. For the purposes of illustration, this handbook uses the crime categories that are used in the Federal Bureau of Investigation's National Incident-Based Reporting System (NIBRS). This system classifies 22 types of offenses as Group "A" crimes and 11 types of lesser offenses as Group "B" crimes. Table 1-2 uses the NIBRS crime categories.

OPEN CASES

Open cases are those in which one or more suspects have not yet been identified or charged, a suspect has been identified but not yet charged, or the investigation is ongoing. As a standard practice, it is recommended that the evidence be maintained by the holding agency for as long as the statute of limitations for the crime or as applicable by law.

> ### Recommendation 1-4:
> Biological evidence that is collected in the course of an open investigation should be retained indefinitely for homicides and, at a minimum, for the length of the statute of limitations for all other offenses.

CHARGES FILED

Standard practice dictates that all evidence in any case being prosecuted is maintained in the event that the evidence is needed for laboratory analysis or court proceedings. When charges are filed, a person has been charged and court proceedings have been or will be initiated. Evidence custodians should be notified if charges have been filed to (1) communicate case status for evidence release requests and (2) assist evidence custodians in determining disposition status.

> ### Recommendation 1-5:
> A communications link should be established between investigators, prosecutors, and the responsible custodial agency to be able to determine if charges are filed.

ADJUDICATED

A case is adjudicated when a final judgment has been rendered in a legal proceeding. The disposition of evidence in adjudicated cases varies according to the crime category. Knowledge of the retention statutes in one's state is essential. Additional guidance is provided in table 1-2. Appendix B identifies evidence retention laws in the United States as a reference.

> ### Recommendation 1-6:
> Biological evidence should be preserved through, at a minimum, the period of incarceration in the following crime categories, as defined in NIBRS, regardless of whether or not a plea was obtained: homicides, sexual assault offenses, assaults, kidnapping/abductions, and robberies. For all other Group A and B offenses, biological evidence may be disposed of upon receipt of authorizations.

UNFOUNDED/REFUSED/DENIED/NO FURTHER INVESTIGATION

In cases categorized as unfounded, refused, or denied, or for which no further investigation will be conducted, evidence can be disposed of upon receipt of disposition approval from the assigned investigator unless such disposal is prohibited by law. This category includes instances in which the victim chooses not to press charges, the prosecutor decides not to file charges, the investigator determines no arrest will be made, or the case is exceptionally cleared.

Recommendation I-7:
After it is determined that charges will not be sought or filed, evidence, including any biological evidence, need not be retained unless destruction is prohibited by statute.

CRIME CATEGORY/CASE STATUS/PERIOD OF RETENTION CHART

In the exercise of his/her duties, the property and evidence custodian may determine the status of cases in his/her custody and may decide whether contact should be made with the investigating officer or prosecutor. Crime categories/classifications vary from state to state; therefore, *knowledge of the specific categories in one's own state is crucial.* Table 1-2 provides guidance.

Table 1-2: Summary of Biological Evidence Retention Guidelines for Crime Categories

Crime Categories (NIBRS*)	CASE STATUS			
	Open[†]	Charges Filed	Adjudicated	Unfounded/ Refused/Denied/ No Further Investigation
Homicide Offenses	Retain indefinitely	Retain indefinitely	At a minimum, retain for the length of incarceration[‡]	Dispose of upon receipt of authorization[§]
Sexual Offenses	At a minimum, retain for the length of the statute of limitations[§]	Retain pending adjudication[§]	At minimum, retain for the length of incarceration[‡]	Dispose of upon receipt of authorization[§]
Assault Offenses, Kidnapping/ Abduction, Robbery				
All Other Group A & B Offenses			Dispose of upon receipt of authorization[§]	

* The Federal Bureau of Investigation's National Incident-Based Reporting System (NIBRS) classifies 22 types of offenses as Group "A" crimes and 11 types of lesser offenses as Group "B" crimes. Table 1-2 uses the NIBRS crime categories.
[†] Cases in which someone was found not guilty after criminal proceedings and additional suspects have not yet been identified or charged should follow the same guidance as open cases.
[‡] Statutes regarding the disposition of biological evidence from homicide, sexual offenses, and other crime categories vary from state to state. Almost all states that have statutes require that such evidence be held for the period of incarceration; a few states require that the evidence be held for the period of probation, parole, or registration as a sex offender. Custodians should check their state statutes. Written authorization for disposal should be obtained from the assigned case investigator. (Note: If the assigned investigator is no longer employed by the agency, a designated investigator should give written approval.)
[§] Section V provides further guidance regarding the disposition process.

II. BIOLOGICAL EVIDENCE SAFETY AND HANDLING

PURPOSE
This section provides guidance on biological evidence safety and handling concerns and includes:

- discussion of universal precautions
- guidance regarding the use of personal protective equipment (PPE)
- guidance regarding exposure control plans
- guidance on the disposal of regulated waste

Individuals handling any evidence should assume that all of it may contain potentially hazardous biological material. Anyone handling biological material may be exposed to harmful infectious diseases. The following section discusses procedural implications related to the safe handling of biological evidence and guidance on the way individuals should protect themselves.

UNIVERSAL PRECAUTIONS
The U.S. Occupational Safety and Health Administration (OSHA) developed universal precautions to protect workers from exposure to human blood or other potentially infectious materials. It is not possible to determine if every bodily fluid or stain collected from crime scenes is contaminated with a bloodborne pathogen; therefore, all bodily fluids and tissues are presumed to be contaminated. When individuals handle any type of biological evidence, procedures need to be in place to reduce or eliminate the risk of exposure to bloodborne pathogens that can transmit disease (OSHA 2012). Common diseases/viruses caused by exposure to bloodborne pathogens include hepatitis and human immunodeficiency virus (HIV). These raise the most concern because of the potential for lifelong infection and the risk of death associated with infection once an individual is exposed.

PERSONAL PROTECTIVE EQUIPMENT
The appropriate use of PPE is intended to protect the individual and the evidence from cross-contamination. PPE includes disposable gloves, disposable overalls, laboratory coats, masks, and eye protection. Every agency should prepare a written policy or directive informing evidence handlers of biological safety concerns and PPE requirements. Directives should include the following universal precautions and work practices, as identified by OSHA (2012), or state regulations derived from OSHA.

- **PPE should be used in every situation in which there is a possibility of exposure to blood or infectious diseases.** Gloves and protective clothing should be worn when providing first aid or medical care, handling soiled materials or equipment, and cleaning up spills of hazardous materials. Face protectors, such as splash goggles, should be worn to protect against items that may splash, splatter, or spray.

- **PPE must be clean and in good repair.** PPE that is torn or punctured, or that has lost its ability to function as an effective barrier, should not be used. Disposable PPE should not be reused under any circumstances. While using PPE, individuals should not touch their eyes or nose with gloves.

- **PPE must be removed when it becomes contaminated and before leaving the work area.** Used protective clothing and equipment must be placed in designated areas for storage, decontamination, and disposal.

- **Dried blood or other dry potentially infectious material should not be assumed to be safe.** PPE should be used when handling these items.

- **When wet material is spilled,** the area containing blood or other potentially infectious material should be covered with paper towels or rags, doused with a disinfectant solution (10 % bleach solution), left for at least 10 minutes, and removed. Materials should then be placed in a waste disposal bag designated for biohazardous material. Appropriate PPE should be used throughout this process.
- **Hazardous biological evidence packages must be appropriately labeled with biohazard labels and signage.** Without the biohazard label (see figure II-1) other employees could inadvertently be exposed to risk or could contaminate the evidence. The labeling and signage guidance also applies to any shelves or rooms where these items are being stored. Additionally, a ventilation system may be required to ensure that employees are working in a safe workplace.

Figure II-1: Biohazard label.

Occupational Safety and Health Administration (OSHA)
OSHA, established by the Occupational Safety and Health Act of 1970, authorizes the Secretary of Labor to develop and promulgate occupational safety and health standards, to develop and issue regulations, to conduct investigations and inspections, to determine the status of compliance with safety and health standards and regulations, and to issue citations for noncompliance with safety and health standards and regulations. The Act also requires that states with an approved state plan provide for the development and enforcement of safety and health standards. Twenty-one states operate their own job safety and health programs (three additional states cover only state and local government employees). States with approved programs must set job safety and health standards that are "at least as effective as" comparable Federal standards. In most cases, states adopt standards identical to Federal ones (OSHA 2012).

OSHA's *Bloodborne Pathogen Standard* is designed to protect the millions of workers in healthcare and related occupations from the risk of exposure to bloodborne pathogens, such as HIV and the hepatitis B virus (HBV). The standard creates numerous requirements for workplaces where workers handle blood or other potentially infectious materials, including bodily fluids.

EXPOSURE CONTROL PLAN
Crime laboratories, property and evidence rooms, and other locations where biological evidence is stored should have exposure control plans in place that are designed to minimize or eliminate occupational exposure to bloodborne pathogens. An exposure control plan is an employer's written policy that outlines the protective measures the employer takes to eliminate or minimize employee exposure to blood and potentially infectious diseases. At a minimum, the plan must contain the following:

- an exposure determination that identifies job classifications and, in some cases, tasks and procedures that involve occupational exposure to blood and potentially infectious diseases
- procedures for evaluating the circumstances surrounding an exposure incident
- a schedule of how and when other provisions of the standard will be implemented, including methods of compliance, communication of hazards to employees, and recordkeeping (OSHA 2012)

Each employee handling biological evidence must be trained on all related requirements and exposure risks.

Agencies should strictly limit the number of employees with exposure to these types of hazardous materials, either through staffing or segregation of biohazardous materials. (See section III for more information.)

BIOLOGICAL EVIDENCE DISPOSAL
REGULATED WASTE

The OSHA standard also defines wastes that should be regulated and monitored. Regulated waste, as defined in *Bloodborne Pathogen Standard*, is liquid or semi-liquid blood or other potentially infectious materials, contaminated items that would release blood or other potentially infectious materials in a liquid or semi-liquid state if compressed, items that are caked with dried blood or other potentially infectious materials and are capable of releasing these materials during handling, contaminated sharps, and pathological and microbiological wastes containing blood or other potentially infectious materials (OSHA 2012).

Regulations governing the disposal of regulated waste or waste that requires special handling exist at the state level, most often from the state's department of health. Generally, state laws require that regulated waste be rendered non-infectious prior to disposal. Once the biohazard is decontaminated, it can be disposed of like any other solid waste.

STAGING FOR DESTRUCTION/DECONTAMINATION

Items to be destroyed or decontaminated must be removed from the active inventory and staged in an area for "bio items" that are scheduled for "destruction" and appropriate disposal.

There are several methods that can be used to destroy or decontaminate biohazardous material.

- **Incineration.** Incineration involves the actual burning of the waste. This method both destroys and decontaminates the evidence. Although effective, incineration is associated with serious air quality concerns. Evidence handlers should consult local and state laws for guidance.
- **Thermal Treatment.** Similar to incineration, thermal treatments use heat to destroy any pathogens present in biological material. There are several types of thermal treatments, such as autoclaves, microwaves, and dry heat systems. Each of these can be used to render biological evidence safe prior to disposal.
- **Chemical Treatment.** The most common method of decontamination is the use of chlorine either in the form of sodium hypochlorite solution (commonly known as bleach) or in the form of the more powerful (and correspondingly more hazardous) gas, chlorine dioxide. These compounds are relatively cheap and effective (HERC 2012).

Individuals responsible for destroying or decontaminating evidence should consult state regulations and the crime laboratory before deciding on an appropriate and safe method for destroying or decontaminating evidence. More information on biological evidence disposition requirements is provided in section V.

III. PACKAGING AND STORING BIOLOGICAL EVIDENCE

PURPOSE

This section provides guidance on the proper packaging and storage of evidence containing biological material. This section includes the following:

- guidance on packaging different types of biological evidence
- high- and low-tech methods to dry wet evidence
- best practices regarding the use of containers and individual item packaging
- guidance on the appropriate conditions for biological evidence storage
- a discussion on storage location considerations
- a list of references for further guidance and training

The packaging and storage of evidence is of paramount importance in forensic investigation. However, requests to produce evidence have demonstrated inadequacies in the packaging and storage of some evidence (Greene and Moffeit 2007; Kiley 2009). Further, studies call for greater care when packaging and storing evidence to prevent contamination and to ensure reliable analysis in the future (Goray, van Oorschot, and Mitchell 2012).

Multiple underlying factors affect law enforcement's ability to appropriately store evidence for optimum preservation, including limitations in the management and capacity of the storage facility, insufficient materials available for packaging, inadequate or improper temporary storage, changes in technology, and the lag between evidence collection and transport of the evidence to the evidence storage facility (Kiley 2008).

The following information will assist those individuals responsible for packaging and storing biological evidence in performing their duties at a level required for optimum preservation of evidence. Nonetheless, jurisdictions should place greater emphasis on the needs of their property rooms and staff members. The jurisdiction must ensure that the agency has sufficient resources and must apply appropriate methods and procedures to ensure that evidence is maintained in a condition suitable for future analysis.

> **Recommendation III-1:**
> In tandem with state or local legislatures, managers in law enforcement and relevant stakeholders should advocate for additional resources and funding to ensure the integrity of biological evidence through prioritizing the packaging, storage, maintenance, and security of the evidence in their jurisdictions.

PACKAGING DIFFERENT FORMS OF BIOLOGICAL EVIDENCE

Biological evidence exists in several different forms, each of which must be packaged, handled, and stored uniquely. Numerous studies have been conducted analyzing the stability of biological material and extracted DNA with varying results. The following guidance uses the expertise of the working group and scientific research to recommend storage conditions and methods that are fit for purpose in light of existing resources available to law enforcement agencies. As technologies advance and DNA testing sensitivities change, more stringent guidelines may be required.

Wet Versus Dry Evidence

There are two physical states in which biological evidence is submitted: wet and dry. Certain types of evidence, such as blood-draw samples or some of the contents of a sexual assault kit, must remain in liquid form. In most cases, these types of evidence are obtained from the crime laboratory or medical facility. All other evidence that is wet should be dried to be properly stored and tested in the future. Drying wet items of evidence, such as a blood-soaked garment, should be the first task of anyone handling wet biological evidence once it has been collected.

Temporary Storage of Wet Items

At times, the evidence handler may have to temporarily store evidence in its wet state because the facilities or equipment necessary to dry it properly are not available. In such a case, the handler should place the evidence in an impermeable and nonporous container (i.e., packaging through which liquids or vapors cannot pass), such as a metal can or glass jar, and should place the container in a refrigerator that maintains a temperature of 2°C to 8°C (approximately 35°F to 46°F) and that is away from direct sunlight. The handler may leave the evidence there until it can be air dried or submitted to the laboratory.

Plastic bags can be used temporarily to store wet evidence but must not be used for long-term storage because of the possibility of bacterial growth or mold. Exceptions include plastic bags that contain desiccant, a drying agent that prevents condensation and the subsequent growth of fungi or bacteria, and breathable plastic bags (Tyvek) that can be used for damp items and swabs.

Methods for Drying Wet Evidence

If evidence with wet biological material is not correctly air-dried, there is a high probability that the biological material will be destroyed by bacterial growth. This could potentially preclude generation of DNA results (National Institute of Justice 2002). Here are a few examples of low-tech and high-tech methods for properly drying evidence.

Figure III-1: Metal lockers used for evidence drying.

Low-Tech

Agencies that do not have sufficient funds or a need (i.e., they do not handle a significant volume of wet evidence) for equipment specifically designed for drying evidence generally use low-tech methods. In these cases, it is recommended that an isolated and secure area—such as a locker, shower stall, or room—be designated for this purpose. For example, a metal locker specifically labeled for biohazards is commonly used to dry evidence. Figure III-1 shows where the submitting officers have attached packaging materials to the outside doors of metal lockers. These materials will be used for repackaging the evidence once it has dried. Wet garments should hang with sterilized paper beneath and between them to minimize contamination while drying. After the drying process, the paper should be packaged separately and submitted with the garment, as it may contain trace evidence.

A shower stall is also an excellent, inexpensive way for departments with limited resources to dry evidence. Departments can create this system with a prefabricated fiberglass shower enclosure elevated on a wooden frame to make room for controlled drainage. (See figure III-2.) If possible,

Figure III-2: Fiberglass shower enclosure.

there should be an adjacent water faucet on which to attach a cleaning hose for washing the enclosure during decontamination.

Any room dedicated to drying evidence should have surfaces that allow for easy decontamination. For example, figure III-3 shows a fully tiled room outfitted with stainless steel hanging rods. The locking mechanism on the door handle prohibits access to all except the assigned personnel.

Figure III-3: Room designated for drying evidence.

Adding complex features to the room, such as a ceiling air filtration system, would move this unit into the "high-tech" category. The drying room should be under negative pressure, with 12 to 15 air changes per hour, and the air should be vented to the exterior of the building (National Institute of Justice and Office of Law Enforcement Standards 1998).

In general, when the low-tech method is used, it is imperative that the area designated for drying biological evidence *not* be in direct sunlight. Additionally, the temperature and humidity should be controlled as much as possible so that the temperature variation is limited to between 15.5 °C and 24 °C (60 °F and 75 °F) and the relative humidity does not exceed 60 percent. Any adjacent areas (e.g., walls, ceiling, and the area below the evidence) should be made of materials that enable decontamination after *every* use of the drying area.

> **Decontamination**
> Decontamination of surfaces or items can be accomplished by using a freshly made solution of 10 percent bleach or a suitable substitute. Individuals responsible for decontamination should consult with the laboratory for suitable substitutes (Centers for Disease Control and Prevention 2012). Refer to discussion on chemical treatment in section II for more information.

Recommendation III-2:
To optimize a sterile environment without commingling items of evidence, property and evidence management should establish a policy or procedure requiring documentation of who is responsible for cleaning the drying area, how the area is to be cleaned and decontaminated, how the decontamination process is documented, and how long the documentation is to be retained.

High-Tech
One of the most acceptable methods for drying biological evidence is the use of a commercially manufactured evidence drying cabinet. The cabinet allows an item to be secured while air is circulated through an activated high-efficiency particulate air (HEPA) filter that draws out any airborne particles. In such cases, the HEPA filter may become evidence as well. This type of equipment generally is found in larger departments and agencies where there is a daily need for drying evidence. (See figure III-4.)

Figure III-4: Commercial drying unit.

Regardless of the type of drying cabinet or locker used, evidence handlers should always place paper under the item to capture any trace evidence that may fall off as it dries. This paper should be packaged separately and submitted with the item. Hangers should not be reused.

If an item cannot be dried, the crime laboratory should provide further guidance.

General Evidence Packaging

If the collected evidence is dry or has been dried, the evidence handler should place each item into a separate, previously unused paper bag or other breathable container. The size and type of container depends on the type of biological evidence. Generally, the bag or container should be securely sealed to ensure that no evidence will be lost (some containers come with manufacturer's seals that do not require tape). As mentioned earlier, all containers should indicate that biohazardous material is stored within the package.

Each package should be labeled with information essential to efficient evidence processing, filing, and retrieving. More information on labeling evidence for tracking purposes is discussed later in this section.

Because packaged evidence may be accessed for testing or examination in the future, materials used to package evidence of different sizes and types should be customized and standardized to properly fit the available storage spaces.

Recommendation III-3:
Each law enforcement agency should develop a protocol for standardizing evidence packaging materials and customizing shelving to allow for more efficient retrieval of evidence stored in property rooms.

Evidence Bags
Homicides, sexual assaults, aggravated assaults, robberies, and burglaries frequently involve bulky evidence, such as clothing and bedding, which presents storage challenges. Figure III-5 illustrates a method that allocates specific shelving for selected sizes of bags and makes each bag easily retrievable. The shelves are no deeper than the longest dimension of the bags, eliminating the possibility of something being hidden behind other evidence. The shelves are designed for two sizes of bags, which are stored by case number.

Figure III-5: Evidence stored in bags.

Evidence Boxes
Another storage option for departments is the use of different boxes sized for the dimensions of the storage shelf. This system uses space efficiently and reduces retrieval time. Evidence stored in boxes with holes (such as handle cutouts in banker's boxes) should be packed in sealed packages. If the evidence is not in a sealable package, the holes of the box in which it is stored should be closed to prevent transfer of any material to another box.

In some cases, firearms are analyzed for biological evidence. Custodians who need to store this kind of evidence should unload the weapon to make it safe and then place it into a new cardboard gun box. The submitting individual must ensure that the box is sealed and must indicate on the exterior of the box that the weapon was unloaded and made safe and may contain biological material. Shelving should be deep enough for only a single box so that one cannot become hidden behind another.

Evidence Envelopes

Small items of evidence (e.g., trace evidence, cigarette butts, fibers, etc.) may be stored in small envelopes. Different sizes of envelopes can be selected based on the dimensions of the shelf or drawers, ensuring efficient use of space and reducing retrieval time.

Figure III-6: Evidence stored in envelopes.

Liquid Evidence, Tissue Samples, Extracted DNA, and Other Types of Evidence Packaging

As stated earlier, certain types of evidence will remain in liquid form or contain fluids. These types require different types of packaging materials as well. Specific storage conditions regarding these and other types of evidence will be discussed later in the section.

Recommendation III-4:
For the safety of employees, agencies should always attempt to segregate types of biohazardous evidence, such as liquid evidence, tissue samples, and extracted DNA, in one centralized location for easy identification and safe storage.

Blood Samples

Generally, blood draw tubes and vials are collected and submitted in some type of container recommended by the crime laboratory and/or hospital. If the department receives a vial or tube that is not packaged in a readily identifiable manner, it should be placed in an envelope that is easily recognizable, clearly marked as to its contents, and bearing a visible biohazard label.

Glass vials of blood should never be frozen because the vial might explode or crack. The Stabilizing Solutions call-out box on page 14 provides guidance on handling and storing vials that contain preservatives.

Hypodermic Needles

Department packaging protocols should require that any type of needle or other sharp object entering the property room be stored in a container that is closeable, puncture-resistant, leak-proof on the sides and bottom, labeled or color-coded, and breathable. An example is shown in figure III-7. These items should not be commingled in a package with other evidence. Sharps containers also must be maintained upright throughout use (OSHA 2012).

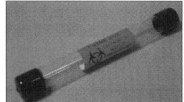

Figure III-7: Evidence syringe tube.

For employee safety, syringes should be stored in an area designated for such evidence. Commingling packaged syringes with other evidence creates a special safety hazard because syringes can accidentally deliver infectious agents directly into the bloodstream (HERC 2012). Filing drawers, bins, or boxes (see figure III-8) can be used for storing these items.

Figure III-8: Storage for tubes or vials.

Urine Samples

If an agency receives a vial or tube that is not clearly labeled as containing urine, it should be labeled or packaged in an identifiable envelope or box that is clearly marked as to its contents. Employee safety mandates that this type of biohazard, similar to blood, tissues samples, and extracted DNA, be segregated in one centralized location for easy identification and safe storage. Urine should not be frozen in glass jars or vials.

Sexual Assault Kits

State or local crime laboratories, local hospitals, or evidence supply vendors generally supply law enforcement agencies with their sexual assault kits. The sexual assault kit packages can be boxes (figure III-9) or envelopes (figure III-10). The contents of these kits can vary by agency. An itemized list of collected items should be submitted with the kit. Boxes and envelopes of uniform size make storage and retrieval efficient, as shown. Given the importance of biological evidence in these cases, sexual assault kits are often retained for decades and must be stored in a manner that prevents degradation and facilitates easy retrieval and identification. Depending on the contents of the kits, a temperature- and humidity-controlled facility may be appropriate.

Figure III-9: Sexual assault kits stored in boxes.

Extracted DNA

Preservation of genomic DNA extracted from biological evidence is an important consideration for any handling, storage, and retrieval procedures, as this DNA may be the only source of material for future testing. Historically, extracted DNA has been stored in a preservative and then frozen or refrigerated. The stability and recovery of DNA extracts is dependent on the quantity and quality of the extracted DNA prior to storage as well as the type of tube used for storage. However, maintaining freezers and refrigerators is costly, which has led to research on room temperature storage of DNA extracts. (Bonnet et al. 2010; Frippiat et al. 2011; Lee et al. 2012; Lee et al. 1991; Smith and Morin 2005; Lee, Crouse, and Kline 2010; Wan et al. 2010). While the Working Group does not endorse a specific method for room temperature storage of DNA extracts, it encourages the audience to consider

Figure III-10: Sexual assault kits stored in envelopes.

such methods as more information becomes available regarding the utility of room temperature storage methods. Contact the crime laboratory to identify what it recommends or requires.

Stabilizing Solutions
In many cases, stabilizing solutions that may eliminate the need to freeze or refrigerate evidence are available on the market to enable easier and more cost effective storage and transportation of DNA samples and other types of biological evidence (Swinfield et al. 2009; Lee et al. 2012; Zhu et al. 2007; Roberts and Johnson 2012). Most crime laboratories use preservatives or stabilizing solutions in biological samples prior to or after testing. Contact the crime laboratory to identify which solution it uses and how this affects the agency's storage requirements.

Tissue Samples
At times, preservation of tissue samples for the long term may be handled by a property and evidence custodian after the tissue has been sampled and analyzed by a crime laboratory or medical examiner. Tissue samples that are submitted for DNA analysis are usually stored at -20 °C as rapidly as possible to halt the degradation process. In cases of mass casualty disasters, freezing or refrigeration may not be immediately available. The use of preservation reagents used to stabilize tissue samples temporarily at room temperature may be advantageous (Graham, Turk, and Rutty 2008; Kilpatrick 2002; Michaud and Foran 2011; Caputo, Bosio, and Corach 2011). The Working Group does not endorse a specific method for packaging or preserving tissue samples because storage methods and preservation reagents vary widely among laboratories. Contact the crime laboratory to identify what it recommends or requires.

Other Items
Items such as a used condom or a fetus (or other product of conception) may be placed in plastic, sealed, and frozen. In all cases where there is some ambiguity in proper storage, evidence custodians should contact the local crime laboratory for further guidance. According to the National Institute of Justice (2002),

> Some methods of collection and storage may promote the growth of bacteria and mold on the evidence. Bacteria can seriously damage or degrade DNA contained in biological material and inhibit the ability to develop a DNA profile; however, evidence can still sometimes yield DNA results. For example, PCR [polymerase chain reaction] technology can allow the laboratory to develop profiles from some moldy biological samples, whereas other evidence may fail to yield a usable DNA profile, even when no mold is visible. Therefore, close consultation with the laboratory is important to determine the type of DNA testing most likely to yield results on the available evidence.

Packaging Best Practices Summary
Agencies should encourage the following best practices in biological evidence packaging.

Containers

✓ Use paper bags, manila envelopes, cardboard boxes, and similar porous materials for all biological evidence. (See page 10 for specific guidance on wet items.)

✓ Use butcher or art paper for wrapping evidence, for padding in the evidence container, and/or as a general drop cloth to collect trace evidence.

✓ Package evidence and seal the container to protect it from loss, cross-transfer, contamination, and/or deleterious change.

✓ For security purposes, seal the package in such a manner that opening it causes obvious damage or alteration to the container or its seal.

Item Packaging

✓ Package each item separately; avoid comingling items to prevent cross-contamination.

✓ Use a biohazard label to indicate that a potential biohazard is present.

✓ Plastic bags are not preferred for storage because of the possibility of bacterial growth or mold.

✓ If drying wet evidence is not possible, place the evidence in an impermeable, nonporous container and place the container in a refrigerator that maintains a temperature of 2 °C – 8 °C (approximately 35 °F to 46 °F) and that is located away from direct sunlight until the evidence can be air dried or until it can be submitted to the laboratory.

✓ Seal each package with evidence tape or other seals, such as heat seals and gum seals; if possible, do not use staples. Mark across the seal with the sealer's identification or initials and the date.

✓ Unload, make safe, and place all firearms submitted into evidence for biological testing into a new cardboard gun box. As the submitting individual, seal the box and indicate on the exterior of the box that the weapon was unloaded, made safe, and may contain biological material.

✓ Label items according to agency policy and procedures. At a minimum, mark each package with a unique identifier, the identification of the person who collected it, and the date of collection. The unique identifier should correspond to the item description noted on the property/evidence report (e.g., evidence tag, property sheet, property receipt, or property invoice). More information on evidence labeling can be found on pages 29 – 30.

✓ Maintain the integrity of the item through the package documentation, including all markings, seals, tags, and labels used by all of the involved agencies. Preserve and document all packaging and labels received by or returned to the agency, because this information is critical.

BIOLOGICAL EVIDENCE ENVIRONMENTAL CONDITIONS

The proper drying and packaging of biological evidence is the first step toward achieving optimal preservation. The next step is storing it in the proper environmental conditions. Biological evidence must be stored in a fashion that not only safeguards its integrity but also ensures its protection from degradation. The storage of biological evidence may include, but is not limited to, the use of temperature- and humidity-controlled areas or freezers and refrigerators. In all cases, it should be understood that conditions of storage should include protection from moisture, excessive heat, and protection from sunlight.

Biological evidence should be stored in one of the following conditions, depending on the type of evidence, and if known, the type of analysis that will be conducted:

- **frozen**: temperature is maintained thermostatically at or below −10 °C (14 °F)
- **refrigerated**: temperature is maintained thermostatically between 2 °C and 8 °C (36 °F and 46 °F) with less than 25 % humidity
- **temperature controlled**: temperature is maintained thermostatically between 15.5 °C and 24 °C (60 °F to 75 °F) with less than 60 % humidity
- **room temperature**: temperature is equal to the ambient temperature of its surroundings; storage area may lack temperature and humidity control methods

Because of the nature of the evidence storage and management process, it is necessary to distinguish temporary storage from long-term storage. In many cases, evidence is stored temporarily because the facility handling it does not have the proper conditions to ensure its integrity for a long time. Temporary storage spaces include medical facilities and hospitals, small property rooms at law enforcement headquarters, or vehicles that transport evidence from the crime scene to long-term evidence management facilities. Throughout this handbook, we define temporary storage to include any location where evidence may be stored for 72 hours or less. Long-term storage is defined as any location where evidence may be stored for more than 72 hours.

Biological evidence stored in a space temporarily has slightly different environmental guidelines than evidence kept in long-term storage because the biological material can degrade over time because of factors that might be less likely to take effect within 72 hours.

The following matrices outline acceptable environments for biological evidence types; however, readers should defer to their crime laboratory's policy. For most situations, the working group strongly urges the use of the guidelines presented here, as they are backed by a comprehensive review of current literature.

Table III-1: Short-Term Storage Conditions Matrix[1]

Type of Evidence[2]	Frozen	Refrigerated	Temperature Controlled	Room Temperature
Liquid Blood[3]	Never	Best	Less than 24 hours	
Urine	Best	Less than 24 hours		
Dry Biological Stained Item[4]			Best	Acceptable
Wet Bloody Items (if cannot be dried)	Best	Acceptable	Less than 24 hours	
Bones	Acceptable		Acceptable	Acceptable
Hair			Best	Acceptable
Swabs with Biological Material		Best (wet)	Best (dried)	
Vaginal Smears			Best	
Feces	Best			
Buccal Swabs			Best	Less than 24 hours

---

[1] Refer to the previous section on "Packaging Different Forms of Biological Evidence" for best practices on packaging types of evidence.

[2] Sources: *Liquid Blood*—Farkas et al. 1996; Austin et al. 1996; Visvikis, Schlenck, and Maurice 2005; Gino, Robino, and Torre 2000; Ross, Haites, and Kelly 1990. *Urine*—Gino, Robino, and Torre 2000; Prinz, Grellner, and Schmitt 1993; Benecke 2004; Elliott and Peakman 2008. *Dry Biological Stained Items*—Gino, Robino, and Torre 2000; Kobilinsky 1992; Lund and Dissing 2004; Sjöholm, Dillner, and Carlson 2007; Aggarwal, Lang, and Singh 1992. *Wet Bloody Items*—Kanter et al. 1986. *Bones*—Kobilinsky 1992. *Hair*—Steinberg et al. 1997. *Vaginal Smears*—Gill, Jeffreys, and Werrett 1985. *Feces*—Benecke 2004. *Buccal Swabs*—Steinberg et al. 1997; Sigurdson et al. 2006.

[3] See call-out box on Stabilizing Solutions for guidance on vials containing preservatives.

[4] This category includes blood, semen, saliva, and vaginal swabs that are dry.

Table III-2: Long-Term Storage Conditions Matrix[1]

Type of Evidence[2]	Frozen	Refrigerated	Temperature Controlled	Room Temperature
Liquid Blood	Never	Best		
Urine	Best			
Dry Biological Stained Items			Best	
Bones			Best	
Hair			Best	Acceptable
Swabs with Biological Material			Best (dried)	
Vaginal Smears			Best	
Feces	Best			
Buccal Swabs			Best	
DNA Extracts	Best (liquid)	Acceptable (liquid)	Acceptable (dried)	

[1] Refer to the previous section on "Packaging Different Forms of Biological Evidence" for best practices on packaging types of evidence.

[2] Sources: *Liquid Blood*—Farkas et al. 1996; Austin et al. 1996; Visvikis, Schlenck, and Maurice 2005; Gino, Robino, and Torre 2000; Ross, Haites, and Kelly 1990. *Urine*—Gino, Robino, and Torre 2000; Prinz, Grellner, and Schmitt 1993; Benecke 2004. *Dry Biological Stained Items*—Gino, Robino, and Torre 2000; Kobilinsky 1992; Lund and Dissing 2004; Sjöholm, Dillner, and Carlson 2007; Aggarwal, Lang, and Singh 1992; McCabe et al. 1987; Kline et al. 2002. *Bones*—Kobilinsky 1992. *Hair*—Steinberg et al. 1997. *Vaginal Smears*—Gill, Jeffreys, and Werrett 1985. *Feces*—Benecke 2004. *Buccal Swabs*—Steinberg et al. 1997. *DNA Extracts*—Yates, Malcolm, and Read 1989; Dissing, Søndervang, and Lund 2010; Halsall et al. 2008; Kline et al. 2002; Sigurdson et al. 2006.

BIOLOGICAL EVIDENCE PHYSICAL STORAGE CONSIDERATIONS

The challenges related to both temporary and long-term physical storage of biological evidence are extensive. In addition to the storage environment, consideration must be given to the proper equipment, safety, training, and management of personnel handling the evidence in a particular physical location.

WRITTEN POLICY

To ensure all submitting officers are presenting biological evidence in a manner that will meet chain-of-custody requirements and/or that will enable proper forensic testing, everyone must follow the organization's established written policies. These policies can come in at least two forms: (1) a *property and evidence room procedural manual* to ensure the required consistency in the overall process, which is made available to all agency staff members; and (2) *written directives* that contain specific instructions for the storage and packaging of biological evidence, which is available to personnel within the property room or unit and evidence submitters.

Policies must clearly state the responsibilities of any employee submitting evidence into the storage system. Typically, these orders would be in the department's general policies, rules and regulations, or standard operating procedures. These policies should apply to every department employee, not only to property room staff members. Rules related to temporary storage, for example, may include the following:

- All evidence collected by any employee should be submitted into the property and evidence system or laboratory by personal delivery to property room or laboratory staff members or, when they are not available, via a locker that has been designated for the temporary storage of evidence. In addition, the evidence should be submitted before the employee goes off duty for that work shift. All evidence should be properly packaged prior to storage.
- Evidence shall not be stored in any unauthorized location, such as a personal locker, desk, file cabinet, or vehicle.
- The submitting employee shall document that the property or evidence is securely locked in the provided locker or temporary storage location.

The policies also should include appropriate packaging methods based upon the needs of the crime laboratory used by the agency and the needs of its own storage facilities. A packaging directive should include digital photos with brief narrative descriptions to best illustrate the approved methods. It is recommended that the servicing crime laboratory be consulted when an agency is developing a packaging directive. These issues also should be considered for temporary storage. Department packaging directives must inform submitting officers on how various types of evidence should be temporarily stored. These directives must include an appropriate contingency plan for times, such as holiday weekends, to ensure items are not left in temporary storage for longer than 72 hours.

RIGHT OF REFUSAL

Departmental policy should clearly state that any package or documentation that does not meet the standards of the property unit or the crime laboratory will be refused, and the submitting officer shall be notified through normal channels to correct the problem. This principle is known as the "Right of Refusal" (Latta and Bowers 2011).

Temporary Storage Equipment
Units used for temporary storage can include commercially manufactured evidence lockers, repurposed lockers, rooms and closets, commercial storage containers, commercially manufactured temporary evidence freezers and refrigerators, home refrigerators, and under-the-counter refrigerators.

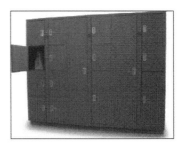

Figure III-11: Commercially manufactured evidence lockers.

Manufactured Evidence Lockers
These include lockers that can be affixed to a wall and unloaded from the front or units built into the wall that can be unloaded from the property room side. Many of the newer, commercially manufactured evidence lockers are self-locking and do not require keys. That is, they have push-shut locks that engage when the door is closed. Figure III-11 illustrates variously sized lockers that can accommodate different sizes of evidence.

Repurposed Lockers
Lockers that were previously used for other purposes can make suitable storage units. However, if padlocks are used to secure the locker, it is best to secure the locks to the locker to ensure they are not lost and to prevent their removal from the facility (which would allow someone to make a duplicate key). Additionally, it is advisable to not use lockers in which the key is left in the locks, because the key could be removed and copied. As stated previously, it is best to select variously sized lockers that can accommodate different sizes of evidence. (See figure III-12.)

Figure III-12: Repurposed lockers.

Evidence Cages
Biological evidence can come in any size and shape. Therefore, lockers and/or cages should be available for large items.

The security of this type of locker must be as strict as that for any temporary locker, and the contents should be cleared out as quickly as possible. As with any temporary storage evidence locker, the larger cage must contain individually packaged evidence from only one case. (See figure III-13.)

Figure III-13: Evidence cages for large items.

Evidence Rooms
Departments sometimes designate a small room, closet, or cage to which all employees have access (e.g., through a key or electronic system) as the temporary storage area for biological or other evidence. If multiple employees have access to the area, it can compromise the integrity of the evidence; be the basis for a chain-of-custody challenge; or result in evidence being commingled or cross-contaminated, tampered with, or stolen. All evidence must be stored in such a manner so that it cannot be commingled or cross-contaminated and so that no one but the submitting officer and the property officer/custodian has access to the evidence.

Refrigerators/Freezers
Some biological items of evidence in temporary storage may need to be refrigerated or frozen at the time of collection and while awaiting receipt by property room personnel. For many years, most departments have used typical residential refrigerator units for refrigeration and/or freezing. A significant concern is the security of the biological evidence during the temporary storage. An additional concern is the potential commingling of evidence from various cases when placed in the same refrigerator or freezer.

Figure III-14: Modified residential refrigerator.

Figure III-14 depicts a typical residential refrigerator/freezer unit in which one agency installed small lockers with padlocks affixed to the frame. Agencies that adopt this method should ensure that padlocks are secured to the lockers and that the entire locker unit cannot be removed from the unit and taken.

Under-the-Counter Refrigerator/Freezer
Small departments also may use an under-the-counter refrigerator unit and install small lockers to segregate items. The locking units shown in figure III-15 are similar to police gun lockers.

Figure III-15: Under-the-counter refrigerator.

The requirements for temporary storage of refrigerated and frozen items are no different from the requirements for any other evidence (e.g., evidence from multiple cases should never be commingled in the same compartment).

Commercial Evidence Refrigerators/Freezers
Larger departments may use larger refrigeration and/or freezer units that can accommodate substantially more biological evidence submissions. The unit in figure III-16 is segmented with individual lockers and can be installed in the wall to allow property room personnel to remove evidence from the back of the unit. These are pass-through lockers and are available as refrigeration or freezer units.

Figure III-16: Commercial evidence refrigerator.

Temperature Alarms
Given the importance of temperature control when storing biological evidence, the refrigerator/freezer unit should be equipped with an alarm system to indicate if there is a rise in temperature and/or an equipment malfunction. The alarm should be monitored 24 hours per day (e.g., by automatic notification to

the watch commander, officer in charge, the communications center, or other designated personnel).

Long-Term Storage Equipment
Generally, when an item is no longer being stored in temporary storage, it is moved to long-term storage. Given the forensic importance of biological evidence in investigations, prosecutions, and post-conviction DNA testing, evidence must be stored in a manner that protects it from degradation and ensures easy retrieval and identification. Allocating specific areas in the property room for the various types of biological evidence can reduce exposure and injuries while also safeguarding the evidence.

Refrigerators/Freezers
Figures III-17, III-18, and III-19 illustrate the types of refrigerators and freezers typically found in most law enforcement agencies.

**Figure III-17
Commercial
refrigeration units.**

**Figure III-18 Labeled
residential
refrigerator/freezer.**

**Figure III-19: Commercial
walk-in refrigeration unit.**

Separating Evidence Types
Property and evidence custodians should consider arranging long-term storage facilities to separate evidence types, such as biohazardous evidence or biohazards ready for destruction. Figure III-20 shows an example of a property room layout that separates biohazards in an area away from and outside the property and evidence facility to enhance security and to enhance protection for staff handling the evidence.

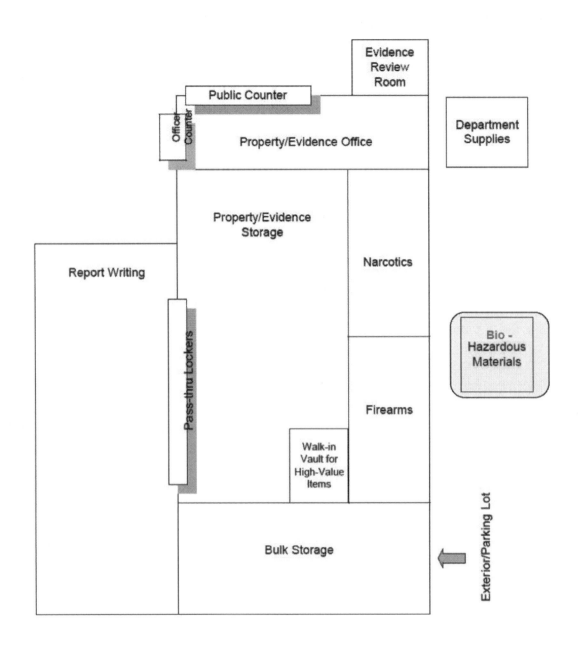

Figure III-20: Sample property/evidence room layout (Latta and Bowers 2011).

IV. TRACKING BIOLOGICAL EVIDENCE CHAIN OF CUSTODY

PURPOSE

This section provides guidance for improving both the chain-of-custody process and the tracking of evidence. This section includes the following:

- guidance on the importance of chain of custody
- best practices for managing and tracking evidence
- a discussion of tracking systems and minimum requirements
- best practices and sample procedures for securing biological evidence
- best practices for evidence management in locations such as a courthouse or hospital
- recommendations on communications and oversight

The justice system requires that proceedings be conducted fairly. A compromised chain of custody can lead to an incorrect verdict. The chain-of-custody record documents the chronological movement, location, and custodial status of physical evidence from the time it is collected through the final disposition. Each person involved with evidence collection, storage, and handling must be able to attest to the condition of an evidence package (e.g., sealed/not sealed or damaged), any changes made to the contents of that package, and the condition of all transfers. Every transfer of evidence between individuals and storage locations must be documented. A break in the chain of custody can be grounds for challenging the admissibility of evidence.

KEY DEFINITION

Chain-of-custody documentation identifies all persons who have had custody of evidence and the places where that evidence has been kept in chronological order from collection to destruction. When done properly, the chain should be an unbroken trail of the collection, custody, control, transfer, and disposition of the evidence. Evidence derived from primary samples—such as DNA extracts from a laboratory analysis—should also have its own chain of custody maintained to the same extent as the original evidence.

Chain-of-custody records may be maintained using a paper-based system, an electronic system, or any combination thereof. An agency that uses a manual system must include a means of tracking the transfer of evidence from person to person or person to storage location. Appendix C contains a sample form to document information that should be obtained by the person collecting the evidence and subsequently recorded for every transfer and transaction in a manual system.

Chain-of-custody documentation should include the following:

- description of the evidence
- unique case identifier (e.g., case number)
- where the evidence was collected
- where the evidence was stored
- who was in possession of the evidence and for what purpose
- what was done to the evidence (e.g., analysis or re-packaging)
- date and time information

Chain-of-custody records must be retained for a period of time, even though the evidence may be destroyed or lost. The specific retention period of the evidence records depends on the type of case and on local, state, and Federal laws.

IMPORTANCE OF CHAIN OF CUSTODY

The chain of custody assists in identifying individuals who may be required to testify regarding the evidence. Failure to maintain proper chain of custody may result in evidence being ruled inadmissible.

Recommendation IV-1:
Personnel who handle evidence should be notified during their training that they might be required to testify about the chain of custody.

MANAGING AND TRACKING EVIDENCE

Scientific and technological advancements have made many more objects available as potential sources of evidence than in the past. The ability to obtain forensic evidence from such sources as blood and other bodily fluids, digital information, and fibers has expanded the pool of evidentiary sources. These evidence categories require special treatment and conditions of storage to prevent deterioration, loss, theft, contamination, mishandling, and improper destruction.

Specific and accurate recordkeeping is essential to knowing the circumstances of the storage, testing, transport, and procedures used in dealing with each category of evidence. Recordkeeping includes chain of custody, security, and quality assurance programs. Records must document how evidence is stored and all persons who have reviewed or had custody of it during storage, such as representatives of the defense, the prosecutor, or law enforcement officials.

The system for tracking evidence must have measures of quality control, must ensure the accuracy of all recordkeeping, and must make it simple to retrieve samples from storage. When selecting a tracking system, an agency should consider that it may need to store the evidence for an extended period of time and that the personnel associated with the case and responsible for the storage and tracking of it may change.

Recommendation IV-2:
Whatever system an agency uses, it should be able to account for the following:
- Chain of custody
    - date/time/identity of individual who collected evidence
    - any person(s) in possession of the evidence at scene and during transport
    - date/time/identity of person who submitted the evidence
    - date/time/identity of property/evidence custodian who accepted/received the evidence
    - date/time/identity of any person to whom the evidence was released and who returned it
- Unique item identification
    - description of item
    - unique number identifier
- Location of item in property/evidence storage room or other external location(s), such as court, a crime laboratory, or another investigative agency
    - location (e.g., shelf number or bin) where evidence is stored
    - date/time/identity of person who stored the evidence

Every item of evidence must have a chain of custody. The tracking system should be able to generate a report accounting for all evidence.

Some cases in the possession of a property and evidence custodian pre-date a labeling system that mirrors the guidance in this handbook. The labeling system for this evidence should be updated as needed on a case-by-case basis.

Each agency should have a standard procedure that governs operation of the property room (Latta and Bowers 2011). This standard procedure should include specific instructions for how and when an inventory should take place as well as who should conduct it.

Recommendation IV-3:
Yearly inventories should be conducted to verify that the evidence in the property room is present and in its specified location.

The removal and return of evidence from storage should also be outlined in an agency's standard operating procedures. The call-out box below is an example of the Los Angeles Police Department's overdue sign-out property procedure.

Los Angeles Police Department (LAPD) Overdue Sign-Out Property Procedure
Within the Los Angeles Police Department, evidence can be signed out on either a temporary or long-term basis. Temporary sign-outs are 7 days and long-term sign-outs are 30 days. Notifications regarding overdue evidence items signed out for temporary or long-term use are handled in a similar fashion and differ only in the time period between notifications (as identified in the chart below). At each interval, notifications are sent to progressively higher management levels within the organization.

Each day, an evidence supervisor queries the property management system for a list of overdue items and makes notifications according to the schedule and format in table IV-1.

Table IV-1: Notification Schedule for Pursuing Overdue Evidence

	First Notice	Second Notice	Third Notice	Fourth Notice
Temporary Sign-Outs	Phone call or email to officer/analyst at 7 days	Email or letter to officer/analyst and his or her commanding officer (CO) at 14 days	Letter to officer/analyst, his or her CO, and the bureau CO via the evidence division's supervising bureau (SB) at 21 days	Letter to officer/analyst, his or her CO, the bureau CO, and the director via the SB at 28 days
Long Term Sign-Outs	Phone call or email to officer/analyst at 30 days	Email or letter to officer/analyst and his or her CO at 60 days	Letter to officer/analyst and the bureau CO via evidence division's SB at 90 days	Letter to officer/analyst, his or her CO, the bureau CO, and the director via the SB at 120 days

It is the responsibility of the various commanding officers to ascertain if the delay is warranted and to send a response to the evidence division or to decide on a course of action for the involved personnel. Each agency must determine its own requirements for return of evidence signed out for investigative purposes.

Recommendation IV-4:
A quality property management system should include a means to identify overdue items or evidence that has not been returned according to the agency's policy.

NUMERICAL IDENTIFIERS FOR CASES AND EVIDENCE ITEMS

Each item of evidence must have a unique identifier, which can take a variety of forms: numeric, alphabetical, a combination of both numbers and letters, or a barcode. Just as with the tracking system, the identification system can be simple or intricate. The key to any such system is that an identifier can never be duplicated and that the item of evidence can be correctly associated with a specific case. An example of such a method would be to assign a unique case number to unique item identifiers for each piece of evidence.

Example 1 uses a case number (2012-12345) plus a consecutive item number.

Case Number – Item Number	Description
2012-12345 – 1	One brown men's shirt
2012-12345 – 2	One pair of men's jeans
2012-12345 – 3	Blood sample from Jane Doe

Example 2 uses the case number (2012-12345) plus the officer's initials (JTL) and consecutive item number.

Case Number – Officer's Initials – Item Number	Description
2012-12345 – JTL – 1	One brown men's shirt
2012-12345 – JTL – 2	One pair of men's jeans
2012-12345 – JTL – 3	Blood sample from Jane Doe

Example 3 uses the case number (2012-12345) plus the officer's employee number (4215) and consecutive item number.

Case Number – Officer's Employee Number – Item Number	Description
2012-12345 – 4215 – 1	One brown men's shirt
2012-12345 – 4215 – 2	One pair of men's jeans
2012-12345 – 4215 – 3	Blood sample from Jane Doe

Example 4 uses a pre-established control number on preprinted, pre-numbered evidence tags/forms that reference the case number. The pre-numbered evidence tags/forms are controlled with a sign-out ledger that carefully tracks each evidence tag/form. The consecutively numbered tags/forms are similar to the management and tracking of traffic citations.

Control Number	Description	Case Number
85123-1	One brown men's shirt	2012-12345
85123-2	One pair of men's jeans	2012-12345
85123-3	Blood sample from Jane Doe	2012-12345

Example 5 uses a computer-generated, consecutive number that is used to document and track the evidence. The computer provides a consecutive number that will never again be generated.

Computer Number	Description	Case Number
789567	One brown men's shirt	2012-12345
789568	One pair of men's jeans	2012-12345
789569	Blood sample from Jane Doe	2012-12345

Recommendation IV-5:
Each agency must develop an identification system so that each item of evidence has a unique identifier. Evidence items created from analysis or separated from the original evidence item should be documented to show the linkage between it and its parent.

KEY CONSIDERATIONS

Location
Tracking the location of the evidence is just as important as identifying the evidence itself. In small agencies, evidence may be stored in only a few lockers, while in larger agencies, there may be many rooms or warehouses, and multiple physical locations. To easily retrieve an individual item of evidence or all of the evidence for a specific case, a tracking system must accurately and consistently provide the location of that evidence. Developing an intuitive scheme for evidence storage makes the system more manageable. Such a scheme may consist of storing like-size containers (e.g., envelopes, bags, and boxes) in areas designed for them and then filing accordingly by the case or tracking number. It is critical that property room personnel update the tracking system with the new information if and when evidence is moved. If not updated, the tracking system will become useless and retrieval of evidence nearly impossible.

Case Status
Another key but often overlooked element to efficient and effective property rooms and tracking systems is the case status. For additional discussion of case status, refer to section V, page 38

Labels
Proper labeling of evidence also is extremely important to a successful and efficient tracking effort. Minimally, the label should include the case identifier, item identifier, type of crime, date/time that the item was collected, where the item was collected, and the name or initials of the person who collected the item. It is also recommended that a description of the item in the package and biohazard labels be included, as appropriate. Any items that contain biological evidence are indicated as such either on the electronic property list or property record.

Many agencies write the labeling information directly on the packaging. Some use adhesive labels with or without barcodes while others may opt for pre-printed packaging. In all cases, the information should be readily available for as long as the evidence is maintained. Therefore, the following points should be considered:

- Are the label and information compatible with the tracking system?
- Is the item uniquely identifiable?
- Is the information on the label legible?
- Will the label adhere to all types of packaging?
- Will extreme temperatures affect the label or its adhesive?

- Is the label format flexible enough to accommodate changes in technology?

If evidence does not bear biological evidence labeling and the presence of biological evidence becomes known, the property and evidence tracking system and label need to be updated to indicate that biological material is contained.

MANAGEMENT AND TRACKING SOFTWARE

Evidence tracking and management software should be able to rapidly identify the following:

- case status
- evidence "out to court" or on temporary release
- evidence "transferred to court" or on permanent release
- evidence pending disposal, release, auction, or diversion
- date/time/identity of responsible person(s) who authorized the release or disposal
- record of final disposition (released, auctioned, destroyed, or diverted), including:
  - specific list of items awaiting destruction
  - name of person authorizing destruction
  - date/time/place/method of destruction and identity of person who destroyed the evidence
  - identity of an independent witness to the destruction
- identity of person who moved the evidence to the pending destruction, auction, release, or diversion storage area with the date, time, and location
- detailed statistical reporting

Additional functions and capabilities to be considered are detailed in appendix A.

Electronic Evidence Management

The increase in the volume of evidence, the budget-imposed decreases in resources available to manage evidence tracking, and the need to track evidence from the crime scene to the courtroom and through final disposition has increased interest and demand for more efficient systems to track and manage evidence. The cost of automated evidence tracking and management software is continually decreasing. In addition, the relatively new introduction of "hosted" solutions (i.e., the evidence tracking and management system is hosted on the vendor's server rather than on a department's server) has enabled many agencies to acquire this level of automation. Thus, evidence tracking and management software is becoming a "must" for an improved evidence processing system.

Management system buyers should consider the following list, in consultation with relevant stakeholders, prior to buying an electronic management to match their process requirements:

- reporting capabilities (including statistics)
- tracking capabilities
- alert mechanisms ("tickler file")
- integration with existing systems
- security
- inventory management
- communication (enhancing data sharing with other criminal justice agencies)

- accessibility (web-based vs. server-based hosted solution)
- usability (ease of use)
- customization (creating a system to meet your needs)
- data conversion
- information technology and hardware support
- training
- appropriate capabilities for the size of agency
- electronic signature capabilities
- cost-benefit analysis for individual features considered (understand value added for each)

AUTOMATED IDENTIFICATION TECHNOLOGIES

Barcoding and radio frequency identification (RFID) are examples of automated systems that aid in the recordkeeping that supports proper chain of custody. Most evidence bagged and tagged at crime scenes is tracked manually by the responding personnel who fill out forms and hand-label the items collected. Many agencies (large and small) use barcode systems to increase the efficiency of tracking evidence, and a few are exploring using RFID technology. Automated systems can also be set up to send alerts to managers when highly sensitive evidence is moved. Some systems maintain photographs of evidence as well. The time-saving benefits and simplified process afforded by an RFID system may be a better value than a barcode system. An RFID system reads many tags simultaneously, whereas a barcode system reads each tag individually.

To obtain more information about the implementation of automated identification technologies, such as barcodes and RFID, the working group engaged a group of consultants to assess the capabilities and technologies available, to review the barriers to their use, and to suggest ways to leverage these systems to increase the forensic evidence visibility. These reports can be found at http://www.nist.gov/oles/.

Recommendation IV-6:
Overall, it is highly recommended that jurisdictions consider automated identification technologies to enhance chain-of-custody recordkeeping and tracking, to facilitate inventories, and to allow for efficient retrieval of evidence.

PROPERTY ROOM MANAGEMENT SOFTWARE

Many law enforcement agencies have purchased property room management software systems that coordinate the intake and storage of evidence in a property room but are not designed to track the return of evidence once it is signed out. This shortcoming can be corrected by using a "tickler" or "flagging" system that indicates when evidence has not been returned by a predetermined time.

LABORATORY INFORMATION MANAGEMENT SYSTEMS

Laboratory Information Management Systems (LIMS) that provide various capabilities for one or more forensic disciplines are available. Since the scope and cost of LIMS vary greatly, the agency or group of agencies implementing LIMS should involve all stakeholders to identify the minimum processes and abilities that will meet everyone's needs. Typically, LIMS cost hundreds of thousands of dollars and are designed to integrate with other systems to manage laboratory instruments and data.

KEY TRACKING SYSTEM CONSIDERATIONS
Level of Integration
There are very few integrated evidence tracking systems available today that will track evidence from the point of collection through storage, processing, and presentation in the courtroom. Many agencies use more than one system to track evidence at different points in the process. The technology is changing rapidly, so considerations of factors such as integration with other systems and methods of accessing data—including web-based platforms—can influence a purchase decision. Some systems can be customized to meet an agency's needs, such as tracking only certain types of data or recording data in a specific format.

Workflow
When choosing a tracking system, agencies must also consider their workflows. Important elements of forensic workflows include maintaining chain of custody, identifying all the data related to a case, and parent/child tracking (e.g., the extraction of a stain to obtain DNA). The systems available today have various capabilities and approaches to providing these capabilities.

Report generation
The final important consideration when selecting an evidence tracking and management system is its ability to generate management reports. A system must have the ability to search, run queries, and print and/or email the resulting data. For example, the ability to run an inventory report for each year in a 5-year span could provide trend analysis that otherwise might be missed. The ability of the end-user, the property room staff members, laboratory staff members, or information technology staff members to customize system reports is a benefit of the more robust and capable systems.

SUMMARY OF TRACKING OPTIONS
There are many evidence tracking systems available, but currently they are focused on specific parts of the process. When transferring from manual to electronic tracking, agencies should procure or develop a system that can manage the entire process—from crime scene to disposition—and not just a portion of the process. Many agencies currently use a manual tracking system for one or more parts of the forensic process and must determine what system is best for them when they consider a new, single system for the entire process using technologies such as barcodes or RFID chips.

As the cost of electronic tracking technologies drops and as integration between systems improves, many agencies that currently manage the forensic process manually will be able to justify purchasing more efficient electronic systems. Prior to procuring new systems, property and evidence custodians, along with other relevant stakeholders, should properly assess the agency's needs.

Recommendation IV-7:
Experienced property and evidence custodian personnel should be included in the procurement of any software and/or hardware that affects the tracking and management of evidence. Agencies need to review existing procedures, to conduct a needs assessment, to develop requirements, and to evaluate technology performance prior to procuring a system. Proper IT support should also be available.

Security
Any location used to retain or store evidence must be secured to prevent tampering, contamination, theft, or contact with unauthorized people. Space should be redesigned as required and security devices must be used.

Recommendation IV-8:
Access to the evidence holding facility should be limited to those who are authorized to remove and return the evidence and to those who are authorized to hand over the evidence to others authorized to receive it. Each evidence custodian should have an appropriate background check prior to employment or assignment to the unit.

When evidence is transferred from one entity to another, public or private, it should either be hand carried or sent via a carrier that maintains an internal, detailed chain of custody with confirmed delivery. Packaged evidence being transferred must be sealed to ensure its integrity. If evidence is opened for examination in a laboratory, during court proceedings, or for any other reason, it must be resealed prior to storing or transferring to another entity. Entities handling biological evidence should establish procedures that include steps to take if evidence is received unsealed. By establishing and following clear and concise procedures, the integrity of the evidence and the chain of custody will be kept intact.

Recommendation IV-9:
Each entity that can potentially hold biological evidence, including courts, should have (1) written procedures detailing the steps and documentation required when evidence is opened, resealed, and transferred; (2) secure, access-controlled locations to store the evidence; (3) trained and authorized personnel handling the evidence; and (4) written policies outlining chain-of-custody and storage requirements (length of retention, conditions, and disposition requirements) for biological evidence.

Courthouse Chain-of-Custody Procedures

There are thousands of courthouses and courtrooms in the United States, and their procedures for tracking and maintaining a chain of custody and storing evidence vary. Because of the need to retain evidence post-trial, it is critical that courts follow guidelines for the storage of evidence. Evidence relevant to a proceeding may be stored and brought to the courtroom from an outside facility, a central property room within the courthouse, or a location designated by a judge. The evidence can be returned to any of these locations when it is no longer needed in the courtroom or when the proceedings are over for the session (Hampikian, West, and Akselrod 2011; Goray, van Oorschot, and Mitchell 2012; Daly, Murphy, and McDermott 2012; Lee, Crouse, and Kline 2010).

When evidence is moved to the courthouse from another location, the courthouse should follow basic chain-of-custody requirements. These guidelines would apply during and between evidence viewings, pre-trial consultations, court proceedings, jury deliberations, and appellate and post-conviction reviews (i.e., anytime an evidence package is opened).

Chain-of-custody records should include a detailed accounting of the following:

- all movements of the evidence package
- any changes to the evidence package, such as opening for a legal proceeding (this should be reflected in the court transcripts)
- the name of the person who has custody of the evidence
- the name of the person to whom the evidence was given
- the purpose of the delivery
- what happened when the evidence arrived at its destination
- the name of the person who returned the evidence to its storage location

After proceedings, including hearings, trial, and jury deliberations, evidence could be stored permanently at a courthouse; however, it is preferable to keep it there only temporarily until court proceedings are completed and then to return it to the submitting agency for disposition.

Guidance on Possible Scenarios
A record of how the evidence package is handled in the courtroom should be reflected in the court transcript. This would include any jury requests to see evidence that would result in changes to the packaging, such as unsealing and resealing. When possible and appropriate, exhibit numbers and case numbers should be cross-referenced in court proceedings.

It is important to have designated locations for evidence storage, whether it is one centralized site for all the judges in a courthouse or a specific area for each judge. A trained court clerk or bailiff for all the judges or separate clerks for individual judges should safeguard the evidence and keep records using uniform procedures and paperwork. The supervising officer should oversee a courthouse's internal chain-of-custody system.

Procedures vary and lines of responsibility are not always clear regarding the repackaging, storage, and preservation of biological evidence after a verdict is rendered or a plea is entered. In some jurisdictions, the evidence is returned to the party who introduced it, while in others, it is returned to a central property clerk's facility.

It is essential to carefully repackage and store evidence once trial court proceedings are completed, as the evidence may be requested again if there are appeals.

To ensure the preservation of evidence post-conviction, it should be properly repackaged and returned as soon as possible to a designated storage site. The documentation accompanying the evidence package should be updated to record the transport back to storage.

Hospital/Medical Facilities Chain of Custody Procedures
Biological evidence should be collected whenever there is the possibility that it may have bearing on a patient's case (e.g., sexual assault, domestic violence, or car accident involving drugs or alcohol) in accordance with state and local laws. Hospitals should develop policies regarding the storage of biological evidence because the hospital and the individual collecting the evidence are involved in the chain of custody. The individual who collects the evidence from the patient is responsible for initiating the chain of custody process. According to the hospital accrediting body, Joint Commission on Accreditation of Healthcare Organizations, hospital staff members who are trained to identify abused patients should also know the procedures for preserving evidence that will support any future legal action.

Recommendation IV-10:
The collection of evidence at the hospital or medical facility establishes the first link in the chain of custody. Biological evidence should be collected by a properly trained medical professional and an inventory of each item should be recorded.

Guidance on Possible Scenarios
If no law enforcement report is made at the time of the hospital/clinic visit, medical professionals should offer to collect evidence from a patient and to store the evidence until the patient or other appropriate person can decide if a police report will be filed. In many cases, there is no specified time period for

which the facility will store the evidence. It is recommended that hospitals establish a specified time period for storage of biological evidence in consultation with the local prosecutor and/or police jurisdiction.

If a law enforcement official does not request the evidence within the specified timeframe, the hospital should contact the patient and seek law enforcement agency authorization prior to destroying evidence. The disposition of the evidence should be documented in the patient file.

If the patient decides to file a report with a law enforcement representative, the medical facility may turn the evidence over directly to law enforcement. In this case, the law enforcement representative is required to sign the chain-of-custody form when taking custody of the evidence from a medical professional at the facility where the evidence was collected.

If the patient has made a report and a law enforcement representative is not available to take custody of evidence, the medical facility can continue to store it or contact the relevant law enforcement agency to request that they handle the storage.

When stored on hospital/clinic premises, dry evidence should be kept in a locked cabinet. It is neither necessary nor helpful to refrigerate dry evidence as stated in the guidance in section II. Wet evidence (e.g., whole blood and urine) should be stored in a locked refrigerator to which only a limited number of authorized persons have access. Those with access can include sexual assault nurse examiners, sexual assault forensic examiners, and the charge nurse or designated supervisor at the medical facility. Evidence should be stored in a secure location requiring a signature for access and removal.

It is not necessary for the same medical professional who collected the evidence to release it to law enforcement. The collector should document that he or she placed the evidence in a locked storage area. When a law enforcement representative comes to retrieve the evidence, the person at the medical facility who turns it over must indicate on the chain-of-custody form that he or she removed the evidence from storage and gave it to law enforcement. The law enforcement recipient also must sign for the evidence and note the time and date of the evidence transfer.

COMMUNICATION

Open, honest, and continuous communication must be maintained among all of the individuals involved in a chain of custody. Stakeholders should be informed of the following: the location of individual pieces of evidence, the status of each case as it pertains to the need for continued storage of evidence, and a consistent case identifier that all entities use and understand.

Recommendation IV-11:
Jurisdictions should work to assess and improve communications regarding forensic evidence by developing consistent procedures and packaging guidelines and by integrating evidence-tracking systems across locations.

OVERSIGHT

To ensure the integrity of recordkeeping and to satisfy chain-of-custody requirements for all biological evidence, jurisdictions should assign a custodian with responsibility for preventing loss, premature destruction, or preventable degradation. The custodian should regularly audit property rooms to ensure adequate security measures are in place, proper evidence-handling procedures are practiced, and proper recordkeeping procedures are followed.

Recommendation IV-12:
Agencies responsible for maintaining biological evidence should assign an appropriate custodian of the evidence to ensure compliance with the recommendations in this report.

V. BIOLOGICAL EVIDENCE DISPOSITION

PURPOSE
This section addresses the proper and efficient disposition of biological evidence and includes the following:

- best practices for the process of evidence disposition
- key elements to include in departmental manuals or polices regarding biological evidence disposition

WHAT IS DISPOSITION?
Disposition is the ongoing process of determining what to do with evidence in a case. The process may entail retention and disposal, destruction, auction, diversion to governmental agency use, or return to owner. Case disposition includes the determination that the legal process is concluded, any further case investigation is completed, statutes of limitation have run for open cases, or no charges will be filed. In some cases, this review process may be performed numerous times. A final evidence disposition is the permanent removal of evidence from inventory after the determination that the evidence is no longer required for any reason. The disposition process is accomplished by anyone responsible for the final determination of the need to retain evidence.

This section discusses general practical considerations for the destruction, auction, or return to owner of biological evidence once the final determination is made that the evidence is no longer needed for any further purpose.

Regardless of the age of the evidence, property and evidence custodians should follow these guidelines prior to the final disposition.

STATUTORY REQUIREMENTS
Most states have laws that provide guidance for the disposition process of biological evidence (see appendix B), but these laws vary widely. This process may include getting a court order, receiving district attorney approval, notifying the law enforcement agency, and/or notifying the defendant/defense attorney or attorneys of record. Before any disposition, it is important to comply with existing laws, policies, regulations, and procedures. Specific detailed guidelines may be available in the applicable jurisdiction or through local, state, and international property organizations.

BEGINNING THE PROCESS
The disposition process can begin in several ways: (1) following adjudication, when the evidence custodian or investigator confirms that all judicial proceedings in the case are completed, (2) when an inventory check identifies evidence that may be appropriate for disposition, and/or (3) when a notification of destruction is sent per statutory requirements.

Some evidence in the possession of a property and evidence custodian will pre-date a labeling system that mirrors the guidance in this handbook. The determination of what contains biological evidence in these circumstances should be made on a case-by-case basis and in accordance with the state policy/statute. Property and evidence custodians are responsible for locating this evidence if further identification is needed.

A release-of-liability document should accompany the release of evidence to the lawful owner. This not only alerts the person receiving the evidence that there is biological material present, but it also may mitigate the risk of liability. Each agency's legal counsel can provide further guidance. This disclaimer can be included on the property receipt.

Each agency should develop a method to routinely review property for disposition. Department policies and procedures need to address the elements of disposition of evidence.

NOTIFICATION MECHANISMS

When possible, every effort should be made to notify all relevant parties during the disposition process. Almost all states that have evidence retention statutes also have mechanisms that authorize destruction prior to the regularly scheduled timeframe. (See guidance for establishing evidence retention requirements in section 1, table 1-2.) These provisions bring all parties' attention to the existence of the evidence and the question of the continued need to retain the evidence. These laws usually require that the holding agency provide advance notice to the court and all relevant parties (i.e., the prosecutor, the defense attorney, and the defendant) and afford an opportunity for the parties to request continued retention of the evidence or to consent to the early disposition of the evidence.

CONFIRMING CASE STATUS

Once it is determined that evidence is no longer needed for any further prosecution or post-conviction proceeding, each agency must act in accordance with its state's preservation of evidence statutes. Some agencies can obtain criminal justice information electronically following the court process. Other holding agencies manually investigate to facilitate the flow of information to begin the disposition process. It is critical that the holding agency determine the status of the case and the requirements of the local evidence retention law prior to the disposition of evidence. Property custodians/evidence personnel may receive notification and authorization for release or destruction in any of the following ways:

- The district attorney's office forwards a case disposition to close, suspend, or reject a case or to return property.
- The court sends disposition on completed cases.
- The property owner inquires about the disposition of his or her property.
- The investigating officer authorizes release or disposal by making a note to that effect on the appropriate property form(s).
- A court order is received ordering release of the property.
- The property, or an accumulation of property, poses a storage problem or hazard, and disposal is ordered by the agency head.
- Department policy allows for property custodians to disposition old items according to the statute of limitations in the Penal Code.

> **Recommendation V-1:**
> Case status reviews should be conducted at least once a year to determine eligibility for disposition of evidence containing biological evidence.

GETTING FINAL SIGN OFF

The agency's investigations unit and/or the prosecuting agency should be the primary decision maker(s) to determine that evidence is no longer needed in accordance with relevant state laws. Sound internal controls should always include the investigating officer's input into this decision. Figure V-1 is an example of a form that can be used to determine method of evidence disposition.

DISPOSITION – REVIEW REQUEST

Date ______________________________

Investigator / Officer ______________________________

Case Number: ______________________________

Control/Bar Code / Item No. ______________________________

Type of Crime: ______________________________

Description of Item: ______________________________

RELEASE / DISPOSE

- ☐ RELEASE ALL ITEMS TO OWNER
- ☐ RELEASE ITEMS ____________ TO OWNER
- ☐ SEND LETTER TO OWNER
- ☐ DISPOSE OF EVIDENCE

RETAIN

- ☐ RETAIN EVIDENCE
  - ☐ CASE PENDING
  - ☐ WARRANT ISSUED
  - ☐ CIVIL CLAIM PENDING
  - ☐ APPEAL PENDING
  - ☐ OTHER ______________________

Signature: ______________________________

Date: ______________________________

Figure V-1: Example of a final disposition review request form (Latta and Bowers 2011).

Recommendation V-2:
Each agency should designate those authorized to sign off on the disposition of biological evidence within a jurisdiction.

Final Disposition of Biological Evidence

Each agency must safeguard and eventually destroy or determine the final placement of all property that comes into its possession. Evidence should undergo final disposition when it is no longer needed; otherwise, property rooms will become overcrowded. Final disposition decisions include diverting, auctioning, physically destroying, or returning the evidence to its rightful owner. When evidence has been seized by a search warrant, a court order may be required prior to final disposition. The final disposition process should document when and how evidence is handled so that any future questions can be answered. Section I offers more detailed guidance on evidence retention rules.

Recommendation V-3:
Timely and proper disposition of evidence is of critical importance in the duties of the property custodian. All property in the care of an agency should be returned to its rightful owner or dispositioned according to law or agency policy.

The checklist below is specific to property and evidence custodians.

Property Custodian Checklist for the Final Disposition of Biological Evidence

✓ Review cases on a regular basis using a "tickler" system, evidence case tracking system, or any of the notification/authorization mechanisms discussed previously that may initiate the disposition process.

✓ Contact the investigator or court to determine case status. The investigator or district attorney should review the case status and determine if evidence is no longer required. Ideally, case investigators should initiate contact with property custodians who have conviction or case information after consulting with the prosecution or district attorney's office.

✓ Get final sign-off from the designated authority to disposition evidence. This authority is determined by the agency's policies and procedures.

✓ Ensure compliance with any statutes, policies, and procedures that may require court orders or notifications before disposal.

   o Private property organizations and state property organizations can offer assistance in preparing policies and can provide information on current legal requirements for property personnel.

   o Be aware of cases with special circumstances that may extend the holding period, including civil lawsuits, death-penalty cases, and fatal accidents.

   o Consult applicable post-conviction DNA testing statutes.

✓ Ensure that final disposition is compliant with state and Federal health and safety laws.

   o If a victim elects to have property returned, return it once it is no longer required by the agency.

   o Verify identification of the owner before releasing property. Adhere to agency policies related to determining ownership.

   o Auction or divert for department use according to law any abandoned or unclaimed items that are of value.

   o If necessary, update or remove from pertinent state or national database systems following disposition any serialized property (items that have individual serial numbers, such as guns, computers, cellular telephones, and vehicles).

Figure V-2 describes steps that agencies should include in evidence disposition, including proper notification, location, and updating of evidence management system records.

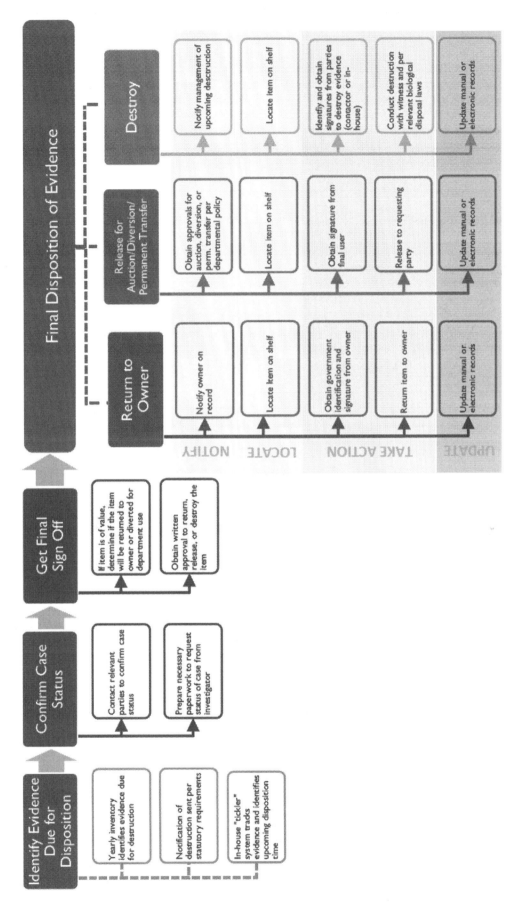

Figure V-2: Summary of process steps involved in biological evidence disposition.

THE BIOLOGICAL EVIDENCE PRESERVATION HANDBOOK

SAFE DISPOSAL OF BIOHAZARDS

Biological evidence poses a hazard for health and safety in the property workplace. Proper handling and disposal methods are vital to maintaining a safe environment. Figure V-3 shows an example of a biohazard disposal bag. Items to be dispositioned must be removed from the active inventory and staged in an area for "bio items" that are scheduled for "destruction" and appropriate disposal. Some states and localities have requirements for biological material disposal. Check with the local crime laboratory for further information. Section II offers more information on biohazard destruction.

Figure V-3: Biohazard disposal bag.

POLICIES/PROCEDURES

The most important task associated with the disposition of biological evidence is to have comprehensive policies and procedures in place to manage evidence disposition.

Table V-1: Recommendation for Property Manual Standard Operating Procedures
(Latta and Bowers 2011)

Recommendations for Property Manual Standard Operating Procedures	
Responsibilities	• Define the property custodian's task and responsibilities in the disposition process • Define the investigator's task and responsibilities in the disposition process • Define other persons in the process, such as a court liaison officer
Research	• Define who is responsible for researching the status of the case • Define the investigator's role in the review and disposition process • Define the prosecutor's role in the review and disposition process
Sign-Off Process	• Define who has authority to sign off property for disposal
Special Requirements	• Define any special handling requirements for cases with firearms, currency, or controlled substances
Time Limits for Review	• Define the time for the review, such as statute of limitations, court disposition sheets, and accelerated reviews
Notification Methods to Investigator	• Define the methods to be used to notify investigator, such as email or formal disposition request forms
Time Limits for Return	• Define the amount of time the investigator has to return the review forms • Define the role supervisors have in the return process
Retention Guidelines	• Define reasons an investigator would need to retain evidence (e.g., warrant issued, case pending, civil case pending, appeal, or statutory requirements)

Recommendation V-4:
An evidence disposition process should be part of each agency's policy and procedures.

SUMMARY OF RECOMMENDATIONS

SECTION I: RETAINING BIOLOGICAL EVIDENCE

Recommendation I-1: All persons who have responsibility for the intake and/or storage and disposition of biological evidence should take online, in-classroom, or other forms of training on evidence management.

Recommendation I-2: Prior to a property and evidence custodian accepting biological evidence, it should be clearly marked and labeled by the submitter as biological evidence, allowing it to be tracked within the evidence management system and stored appropriately from intake through disposition.

Recommendation I-3: Property and evidence custodians should consult with investigators, laboratory analysts, and, when appropriate, prosecutors to determine whether only representative sample(s) should be retained in situations in which samples are too large or too costly to store. Property and evidence custodians, investigators, laboratory analysts, and prosecutors should discuss situations in which prosecutors should be consulted. These decisions should not be made exclusively by property and evidence custodians.

Recommendation I-4: Biological evidence that is collected in the course of an open investigation should be retained indefinitely for homicides and, at a minimum, for the length of the statute of limitations for all other offenses.

Recommendation I-5: A communications link should be established between investigators, prosecutors, and the responsible custodial agency to be able to determine if charges are filed.

Recommendation I-6: Biological evidence should be preserved through, at a minimum, the period of incarceration in the following crime categories, as defined in NIBRS, regardless of whether or not a plea was obtained: homicides, sexual assault offenses, assaults, kidnapping/abductions, and robberies. For all other Group A and B offenses, biological evidence may be disposed of upon receipt of authorizations.

Recommendation I-7: After it is determined that charges will not be sought or filed, evidence, including any biological evidence, need not be retained unless destruction is prohibited by statute.

SECTION III: PACKAGING AND STORING BIOLOGICAL EVIDENCE

Recommendation III-1: In tandem with state or local legislatures, managers in law enforcement and relevant stakeholders should advocate for additional resources and funding to ensure the integrity of biological evidence through prioritizing the packaging, storage, maintenance, and security of the evidence in their jurisdictions.

Recommendation III-2: To optimize a sterile environment without commingling items of evidence, property and evidence management should establish a policy or procedure requiring documentation of who is responsible for cleaning the drying area, how the area is to be cleaned and decontaminated, how the decontamination process is documented, and how long the documentation is to be retained.

Recommendation III-3: Each law enforcement agency should develop a protocol for standardizing evidence packaging materials and customizing shelving to allow for more efficient retrieval of evidence stored in property rooms.

Recommendation III-4: For the safety of employees, agencies should always attempt to segregate types of biohazardous evidence, such as liquid evidence, tissue samples, and extracted DNA, in one centralized location for easy identification and safe storage.

Recommendation III-5: Each law enforcement agency should have a policy and procedure for the storage of biological evidence.

SECTION IV: TRACKING BIOLOGICAL EVIDENCE CHAIN OF CUSTODY

Recommendation IV-1: Personnel who handle evidence should be notified during their training that they might be required to testify about the chain of custody.

Recommendation IV-2: Whatever system an agency uses, it should be able to account for the following:
- Chain of custody
    - date/time/identity of individual who collected evidence
    - any person(s) in possession of the evidence at scene and during transport
    - date/time/identity of person who submitted the evidence
    - date/time/identity of property/evidence custodian who accepted/received the evidence
    - date/time/identity of any person to whom the evidence was released and who returned it
- Unique item identification
    - description of item
    - unique number identifier
- Location of item in property/evidence storage room or other external location(s), such as court, a crime laboratory, or another investigative agency
    - location (e.g., shelf number or bin) where evidence is stored
    - date/time/identity of person who stored the evidence

Recommendation IV-3: Yearly inventories should be conducted to verify that the evidence in the property room is present and in its specified location.

Recommendation IV-4: A quality property management system should include a means to identify overdue items or evidence that has not been returned according to the agency's policy.

Recommendation IV-5: Each agency must develop an identification system so that each item of evidence has a unique identifier. Evidence items created from analysis or separated from the original evidence item should be documented to show the linkage between it and its parent.

Recommendation IV-6: Overall, it is highly recommended that jurisdictions consider automated identification technologies to enhance chain-of-custody recordkeeping and tracking, to facilitate inventories, and to allow for efficient retrieval of evidence.

Recommendation IV-7: Experienced property and evidence custodian personnel should be included in the procurement of any software and/or hardware that affects the tracking and management of evidence. Agencies need to review existing procedures, to conduct a needs assessment, to develop requirements, and to evaluate technology performance prior to procuring a system. Proper IT support should also be available.

Recommendation IV-8: Access to the evidence holding facility should be limited to those who are authorized to remove and return the evidence and to those who are authorized to hand over the evidence to others authorized to receive it. Each evidence custodian should have an applicable background check prior to employment or assignment to the unit.

Recommendation IV-9: Each entity that can potentially hold biological evidence, including courts, should have (1) written procedures detailing the steps and documentation required when evidence is opened, resealed, and transferred; (2) secure, access-controlled locations to store the evidence; (3) trained and authorized personnel handling the evidence; and (4) written policies outlining chain-of-custody and storage requirements (length of retention, conditions, and disposition requirements) for biological evidence.

Recommendation IV-10: The collection of evidence at the hospital or medical facility establishes the first link in the chain of custody. Biological evidence should be collected by a properly trained medical professional and an inventory of each item should be recorded.

Recommendation IV-11: Jurisdictions should work to assess and improve communications regarding forensic evidence by developing consistent procedures and packaging guidelines and by integrating evidence-tracking systems across locations.

Recommendation IV-12: Agencies responsible for maintaining biological evidence should assign an appropriate custodian of the evidence to ensure compliance with the recommendations in this report.

SECTION V: BIOLOGICAL EVIDENCE DISPOSITION

Recommendation V-1: Case status reviews should be conducted at least once a year to determine eligibility for disposition of evidence containing biological evidence.

Recommendation V-2: Each agency should designate those authorized to sign off on the disposition of biological evidence within a jurisdiction.

Recommendation V-3: Timely and proper disposition of evidence is of critical importance in the duties of the property custodian. All property in the care of an agency should be returned to its rightful owner or dispositioned according to law or agency policy.

Recommendation V-4: An evidence disposition process should be part of each agency's policy and procedures.

APPENDIX A: EVIDENCE TRACKING AND MANAGEMENT SYSTEMS: FUNCTIONS, CAPABILITIES, AND REPORTS TO BE CONSIDERED WHEN ACQUIRING A NEW SYSTEM

The table below is adapted from *Property and Evidence by the Book* (Latta and Bowers 2011).

Item #	Item	Comment
	**EVIDENCE TRACKING AND MANAGEMENT SYSTEMS** Functions, Capabilities, Reports, etc. To be considered when acquiring a new system	
1	**HARDWARE/OPERATING SYSTEM**	
1.1	Browser-based system	Does the operating system use standard browsers?
1.2	Export features	Does the system provide easy export of data?
1.3	Maximum number of items	Are there an unlimited number of items that can be entered and tracked by the system?
1.4	Number of users	How many users does the system permit (e.g., an unlimited number of users)?
1.5	Type of server used by the provider	What type of server does the system provider use (e.g., SQL, Oracle)?
1.6	Server—robust and crash resistant	What is the history of the type of server that is being used by the system provider?
1.7	Data backup	Is the data from your system automatically backed up? If not, is backup a simple task?
1.8	Default event process for crashes	What is the default function if the system crashes?
1.9	User friendliness of the system	Is the functionality, such as report generation, user friendly for the property and evidence custodian, property manager, etc.?
2.0	**INSTALLATION AND INTEGRATION**	
2.1	Company history	How many years has the system provider been offering this type of system?
2.2	Number of clients	How many law enforcement agencies are currently using this system for property and evidence tracking and management?
2.3	Implementation: modular or entire system	When the system is being implemented, is it done one module at a time, or is the entire system implemented simultaneously?

2.4	Commercial Off the Shelf (COTS) system	Is this available as a COTS system?
2.5	INTEGRATIONS	
2.5.1	Integration with Laboratory Information Management System (LIMS)	Can this system be integrated with LIMS?
2.5.2	History of integration with LIMS	How many agencies have integrated the provider's system with LIMS?
2.5.3	Integration with a Records Management System (RMS)	Can this system be integrated with an RMS?
2.5.4	History of integration with RMS	How many agencies have integrated the provider's system with an RMS?
2.5.5	Microsoft Word and Excel integration	Does the system integrate with both Microsoft Word and Excel for report generation, correspondence, etc.?
3.0	**REPORTING FUNCTIONALITY**	
3.1	Standard and user-customized reports	Can the system produce standard and user-customized reports for both internal management and external reporting purposes?
3.1.1	Chain-of-custody reports	
3.1.2	Auction reports	
3.1.3	Letters to owners of property	
3.1.4	Inventory reports	
3.1.5	Firearms staged for destruction	Awaiting destruction
3.1.5.1	Firearms destruction list	After the actual destruction
3.1.6	Narcotics staged for destruction	Awaiting destruction
3.1.6.1	Narcotics destruction list	After the actual destruction
3.1.9	Currency ready for transfer	Awaiting transfer to bank or other financial institution
3.1.9.1	Currency transfer list	After the actual transfer
3.2	Crystal reports	Is the system capable of producing crystal reports?
3.3	Disposition notices	Can the system produce disposition notices (i.e., documents sent to an investigator who is authorized to dispose)?
3.3.1	Disposition notices—user-configurable queries	Can the disposition notices be generated based on user-configurable queries?
3.4	TICKLER FILES—Customizable	Can the system create user-customizable tickler files?

3.4.1	Items pending destruction reports	
3.4.2	Items pending auction reports	
3.4.3	Currency pending transfer to bank or other financial institution	
3.4.4	Property awaiting owner pick-up	
3.4.5	Items out to the crime laboratory	
3.4.6	Items out to court	
3.4.7	Items out to investigator/officer	
3.4.8	Items out to other agency	
3.5	OTHER REPORTS	
3.5.1	National Crime Information Center (NCIC) searches	Can the system conduct NCIC searches and maintain an audit trail of all searches?
3.5.2	Currency accounting ledger	Will the system record currency accounting actions, such as intake, current balance, and transfer?
3.5.3	Inventory history	Will the system maintain an inventory history, including the date, conducted by, total items, total firearms, total narcotics, total currency on hand, and "exception" (also known as "discrepancy") reports?
3.5.4	User-definable and editable fields	Does the system enable users to define and/or edit fields, such as creating a storage location of "guns ready for destruction," "narcotics ready for destruction," and "currency ready for transfer"? Does the system enable the user to customize by including crime code numbers so that the entry of a number will automatically convert it to the name of the crime category? (For example, a department in California enters "187" and the system automatically converts that to read "homicide" for the category field.)
4.0	**TRACKING**	
4.1	Create a "hold" for an item	Can the user place a "hold" on an item based on a pending appeal process and/or the request of an investigator or prosecutor?
4.2	Link item to other cases	Can the user link a single item of evidence to multiple cases to ensure that it is not disposed of until all related cases are closed and disposition is received?

4.3	Attach digital image	Can the system attach digital images and/or electronic reports (photos, reports, signature captures, Government ID scans, etc.) to the record for the item?
4.4	Global move (batch move)	Can multiple items be moved within the system from one location to another location (e.g., from the "pending destruction" location to the final location of "destroyed")?
5.0	**INVENTORIES AND AUDITS**	
5.1	Use of portable barcode scanners	Does the system enable an inventory to be conducted using barcodes and barcode scanners?
5.2	Use of Radio Frequency Identification Devices (RFID)	Does the system enable an inventory to be conducted using RFID technology?
5.3	Exception reports	Are "exception" (also known as "discrepancy") reports generated based on the barcode or RFID scan of the inventory in individual and/or multiple storage locations?
5.4	Inventory lists by location	Can the user create and print inventory lists of items by individual storage locations within the property room/warehouse?
5.5	Audit lists	Can the system generate a list of randomly selected items for an audit?
6.0	**SECURITY**	
6.1	Access control to tracking system	Can the user customize security access and/or functions to individuals (e.g., "read only" access, "restricted access to certain fields of data," or "full access to system")?
6.2	Encryption	If the service provider is a hosted solution (i.e., the provider maintains all of the data on its servers), is there Secure Socket Layer (SSL) encryption and security?
7.0	**BARCODES, RFID, RELATED ITEMS**	
7.1	Use of barcodes—tracking	Does the system use barcodes for tracking?
7.1.1	Use of barcodes—inventory	Does the system use barcodes for inventory?
7.1.2	Use of barcodes—audits	Does the system use barcodes for audits?
7.2	Customized item labels with barcodes	Can the user create customized packaging labels that contain desired information about the item as well as a barcode?
7.3	Thermal printers	Does the system provider offer thermal printers for the customized packaging labels?

	Barcode scanners	Does the system provide wired and/or portable wireless barcode scanners?
7.4	Use of RFID—tracking	Does the system use RFID for tracking?
7.4.1	Use of RFID—inventory	Does the system use RFID for inventory?
7.4.2	Use of RFID—audits	Does the system use RFID for audits?
8.0	**TRAINING**	
8.1	Onsite training	Does the system provider offer onsite training on the system?
8.2	Refresher training	Does the system provider offer refresher training on the system?
8.2.1	Web-based training	Is training offered online and on demand by specific system components, capabilities, functions, etc.?
8.3	New employee training	What training is available from the system provider for newly hired/transferred property and evidence custodians (e.g., training on what the system does and how to use it)?

APPENDIX B: LIST OF EVIDENCE RETENTION LAWS

State	Statute/Case Law	Effective Year; Amendments	Crime Categories
ALABAMA	Ala. Code 1975 § 15-18-200	2009	capital offense
ALASKA	A.S. § 12.36.200	2010	murder, manslaughter, criminally negligent homicide, first degree sexual assault, first degree sexual abuse of a minor
ARIZONA	A.R.S. § 13-4221	2009	homicide or felony sexual offense
ARKANSAS	A.C.A. § 12-12-104	2001; 2011	sex offense, violent offense, felony for which the state may take the defendant's DNA for the state's database
CALIFORNIA	Penal Code § 1417.9	2000; 2001, 2002	all criminal cases
COLORADO	C.R.S.A. § 18-1-1101, et seq.	2009	any felony or sex offense
CONNECTICUT	C.G.S.A. § 54-102jj	2003	capital felony and any crime where a person was convicted at trial, or upon order of the court for good cause shown
DELAWARE	None	n/a	n/a
DISTRICT OF COLUMBIA	DC ST § 22-4134	2002	crime of violence
FLORIDA	F.S.A. § 925.11	2001; 2004; 2006	Felony
GEORGIA	Ga. Code Ann. § 17-5-56	2003; 2008; 2011	criminal case
HAWAII	HRS § 844D-126	2005	case in which there has been a judgment of conviction
IDAHO	None	n/a	n/a
ILLINOIS	725 ILCS 5/116-4	2001; 2010	homicide, sexual offenses (aggravated criminal sexual assault, criminal sexual assault, predatory sexual assault on a child, aggravated criminal sexual abuse, criminal sexual abuse), attempts, any felony for which genetic profile may be added to database
INDIANA	Ind. Code. Ann. 35-38-7-14	2001	murder and class A, B, and C felonies
IOWA	I.C.A. § 81.10	2005	criminal actions
KANSAS	K.S.A. § 21-2512	2001	murder and rape

KENTUCKY	Ky. Rev. Stat. Ann. § 524.140	2002; 2007	capital crimes, all class A, B, C felonies, certain D felonies (sexual offenses) cf. "the appropriate governmental entity shall retain any biological material secured in connection with <u>a criminal case</u> for the period of time that any person remains incarcerated in connection with that case."
LOUISIANA	La. Code Crim. Proc. Ann. art. 926.1; HB 116 (2011)	2001; 2003; 2006; 2008; 2011	felonies; convictions after trial or Alford plea for homicide, rape, armed robbery are subject to moratorium on destruction (in HB 116)
MAINE	15 M.R.S.A. § 2138	2001, 2005, 2006	any crime carrying the potential punishment of at least one year imprisonment (felonies)
MARYLAND	MD Code of Crim. Proc. § 8-201	2001; 2002; 2003; 2004; 2008; 2014	murder (1st and 2nd degree); manslaughter; rape (1st and 2nd degree); sexual offense (1st and 2nd degree)
MASSACHUSETTS	2012 Mass. Legis. Serv. Ch. 38 (S.B. 1987) (WEST)	2011	Criminal offense
MICHIGAN	Mich. Comp. Laws Ann. § 770.16	2001; 2005; 2009	felony
MINNESOTA	M.S.A. § 590.10	2005	criminal case
MISSISSIPPI	Miss. Code Ann. § 99-49-1	2009	Crime
MISSOURI	V.A.M.S. 650.056	2001; 2006	felony for which defendant's DNA may be collected for entry into the state database (effect is all felonies)
MONTANA	Mont. Code Ann. §46-21-111	2003; 2009	Felony
NEBRASKA	Neb.Rev.St. § 29-4125	2001; 2003; 2007	criminal case
NEVADA	Nev. Rev. Stat. § 176.0912	2009	category A or B felony
NEW HAMPSHIRE	N.H. Rev. Stat. § 651-D:3	2004	a criminal or delinquency investigation or prosecution
NEW JERSEY	None	n/a	n/a
NEW MEXICO	N.M. Stat. Ann. §31-1A-2	2003; 2005	Felony
NEW YORK	None	n/a	n/a

NORTH CAROLINA	N.C.G.S.A. § 15A-268	2001; 2008; 2009	class A – E felonies (death sentences, violent offenses, offense requiring sex offender registration, all other felonies) – "Notwithstanding any other provision of law and subject to subsection (b) of this section, a custodial agency shall preserve any physical evidence that is reasonably likely to contain any biological evidence collected in the course of a criminal investigation or prosecution."
NORTH DAKOTA	None	n/a	n/a
OHIO	Ohio Rev. Code Annot. § 2933.82	2010	aggravated murder, murder, voluntary manslaughter, first or second degree involuntary manslaughter, first or second degree vehicular manslaughter, rape, attempted rape, sexual battery, gross sexual imposition of a person under 13
OKLAHOMA	22 Okl. St. Ann. § 1372	2001	violent felony offense
OREGON	OR SB 731	2011	aggravated murder, murder, rape in the first degree, sodomy in the first degree, unlawful sexual penetration in the first degree, aggravated vehicular homicide, manslaughter in the first degree or manslaughter in the second degree
PENNSYLVANIA	Pa. Stat. Ann. 42 § 9543.1	2002	criminal offense
RHODE ISLAND	RI ST § 10-9.1-11	2002	any crime

SOUTH CAROLINA	SC Code 1976 § 17-28-310, et seq.	2009	murder; killing by poison; killing by stabbing or thrusting; voluntary manslaughter; homicide by child abuse; aiding and abetting a homicide by child abuse; lynching; killing in a dual; spousal sexual battery; criminal sexual conduct in the first second or third degree; criminal sexual conduct with a minor; arson in the first degree; burglary or armed robbery in first degree carrying a sentence of more than 10 years; abuse or neglect of a vulnerable adult resulting in death; sexual misconduct with an inmate, patient or offender; unlawful removing or damage of an airport facility resulting in death; interference with traffic control devices or railroad signs or signals resulting in death; driving a motor vehicle under the influence of drugs or alcohol resulting in death; obstruction of a railroad resulting in death; or accessory before the fact in any of the enumerated offenses.
SOUTH DAKOTA	SDCL § 23-5B-5	2009	Felony
TENNESSEE	Tenn. Code Ann. § 40-30-309	2001	first degree murder, second degree murder, aggravated rape, rape, aggravated sexual battery or rape of a child, attempt
TEXAS	Texas C.C.P. Art. 38.43	2001; 2009; 2011	Felony
UTAH	U.C.A. 1953 § 78B-9-301	2008; 2011	Felony
VERMONT	None	n/a	n/a
VIRGINIA	Va. Code Ann. § 19.2-270.4:1	2001; 2002; 2005	Felony
WASHINGTON	West's RCWA 10.73.170	2000; 2001; 2003; 2005	Felony
WEST VIRGINIA	None	n/a	n/a
WISCONSIN	W.S.A. §§ 165.81, 757.54, 968.205, 978.08	2001; 2005	crime
WYOMING	W.S.1977 § 7-12-304	2008	Crime

APPENDIX C: SAMPLE CHAIN-OF-CUSTODY REPORT

Property Record Number:
_____

Anywhere Police Department

EVIDENCE CHAIN OF CUSTODY TRACKING FORM

Case Number: _____ Offense: _____
Submitting Officer: (Name/ID#) _____
Victim: _____
Suspect: _____
Date/Time Seized: _____ Location of Seizure: _____

Description of Evidence		
Item #	**Quantity**	**Description of Item** (Model, Serial #, Condition, Marks, Scratches)

Chain of Custody				
Item #	**Date/Time**	**Released by** (Signature & ID#)	**Received by** (Signature & ID#)	**Comments/Location**

APD_Form_#PE003_v.1 (12/2012)   Page 1 of 2 pages (See back)

EVIDENCE CHAIN-OF-CUSTODY TRACKING FORM
(Continued)

Chain of Custody				
Item #	Date/Time	Released by (Signature & ID#)	Received by (Signature & ID#)	Comments/Location

Final Disposal Authority

Authorization for Disposal

Item(s) #: _____ on this document pertaining to (suspect): _____
is(are) no longer needed as evidence and is/are authorized for disposal by (check appropriate disposal method)
☐ Return to Owner   ☐ Auction/Destroy/Divert
Name & ID# of Authorizing Officer: _____ Signature: _____ Date: _____

Witness to Destruction of Evidence

Item(s) #: _____ on this document were destroyed by Evidence Custodian _____ ID#:_____
in my presence on (date) _____.
Name & ID# of Witness to destruction: _____ Signature: _____ Date: _____

Release to Lawful Owner

Item(s) #: _____ on this document was/were released by Evidence Custodian _____
_____ ID#:_____ to
Name _____
Address: _____ City: _____ State: _____ Zip Code: _____

Telephone Number: (____) _____
Under penalty of law, I certify that I am the lawful owner of the above item(s).

Signature: _____ Date: _____

Copy of Government-issued photo identification is attached. ☐ Yes ☐ No

This Evidence Chain-of-Custody form is to be retained as a permanent record by the Anywhere Police Department.

GLOSSARY

This glossary provides a guide in the interpretation and understanding of the document. When possible, definitions were selected from existing references. Certain definitions were specifically crafted to elucidate the intent of the document.

Biohazards: Materials that contain blood or other potentially infectious materials. These materials include many of those found in biological evidence, including semen, vaginal secretions, or any bodily fluid that is visibly contaminated with blood, and all bodily fluids in situations in which it is difficult or impossible to differentiate between bodily fluids as well as any unfixed tissue or organ from a human (living or dead) that can be collected at a crime scene and stored (OSHA 2012).

Biological Evidence: Samples of biological material—such as hair, tissue, bones, teeth, blood, semen, or other bodily fluids—or evidence items containing biological material (DNA Initiative 2012).

Bloodborne Pathogens: Microorganisms that are present in human blood and can cause disease in humans. These pathogens include, but are not limited to, hepatitis B virus and human immunodeficiency virus (OSHA 2012).

Chain of Custody: Identification of the person or agency having custody of evidence and the place where that evidence is kept, in chronological order from the time evidence is collected to its destruction. A formal, written process that records the persons having custody of evidence from initial point of receipt or custody by a representative of a law enforcement agency to its final disposition by the agency. The record also reflects the dates and reasons evidence is transferred from one location or person to another. A chain-of-custody record could also be included in a court transcript.

Exceptionally Cleared: A case status where an offender is not arrested and formally charged due to some element beyond law enforcement control. Examples of exceptional clearances include, but are not limited to, the death of the offender (e.g., suicide or justifiably killed by police or citizen); the victim's refusal to cooperate with the prosecution after the offender has been identified; or the denial of extradition because the offender committed a crime in another jurisdiction and is being prosecuted for that offense (Federal Bureau of Investigation, 2013).

Contamination: The unwanted transfer of material from another source to a piece of physical evidence (National Institute of Justice "Crime Scene Investigation: A Guide for Law Enforcement" 2000).

Crime Laboratory: A facility (Government or private) that analyzes physical evidence.

Crime Scene: A location in which (or a person upon who) a crime may have occurred.

Degradation: The transition from a higher to a lower level of quality.

Desiccant: A substance used as a drying agent.

DNA: The genetic material; a double helix composed of two complementary chains of paired bases (nucleotides) (National Institute of Justice "The Future of Forensic DNA Testing: Predictions of the Research and Development Working Group" 2000); deoxyribonucleic acid (DNA), often referred to as the "blueprint of life," it is the genetic material present in the nuclei of cells that is inherited, half from each biological parent. DNA is a chemical substance contained in cells that determines each person's individual characteristics. An individual's DNA is unique, except in cases of identical twins.

<u>Dried Down</u>: Evidence that has been fully dried so that no liquid (e.g., blood, semen) can drip from the object.

<u>Evidence</u>: Property that may be related to a crime and/or that may implicate a person in or clear a person of a crime.

<u>Evidence Collector</u>: The person who initially took ownership of an item for evidentiary purposes.

<u>Evidence Custodian</u>: The person who is responsible for evidence processing in a given location (e.g., property and evidence room, hospital, court, crime laboratory). This person can be an evidence collector or handler as well.

<u>Evidence Handler</u>: Any person who has had evidence in his or her possession at any given time. A record of this handler must be kept in the chain-of-custody record.

<u>Evidence Packaging</u>: The manner in which items with potential evidentiary value are wrapped, bagged, or boxed to be preserved, documented, and labeled (Latta and Bowers 2011).

<u>Extracted DNA</u>: Genomic DNA extracted from biological evidence; DNA in its raw form.

<u>First Responder</u>: The initial responding law enforcement officer(s) and/or other public safety official(s) or service provider(s) arriving at the scene before the arrival of the investigator(s) in charge (National Institute of Justice "Crime Scene Investigation: A Guide for Law Enforcement" 2000).

<u>Frozen</u>: A storage condition in which the temperature is maintained thermostatically at or below $-10°C$ (14°F).

<u>Hepatitis B</u>: A viral disease that causes inflammation of the liver and is primarily spread through exposure to infectious blood or bodily fluids, such as semen and vaginal secretion.

<u>Hepatitis C</u>: A viral disease that causes inflammation of the liver and is primarily spread through blood-to-blood contact.

<u>High-Efficiency Particulate Air (HEPA) Filter</u>: A filter that satisfies U.S. Department of Energy standards of efficiency and removes 99.97% of all particles greater than 0.3 micrometer from the air that passes through.

<u>Human Immunodeficiency Virus (HIV)</u>: A virus that causes a condition in humans that leads to the progressive failure of the immune system and can be spread by the transfer of blood, semen, vaginal fluid, pre-ejaculate, or breast milk.

<u>Integrated Software Systems</u>: A collection of computer programs designed to work together to handle an application, either by passing data from one to another or as components of a single system. Integrated systems may include Computer Aided Dispatch, Records Management System, Laboratory Information Management System, and Property Evidence Module.

<u>Law Enforcement Agency</u>: Any agency that enforces the law. This may be local or state police or Federal agencies, such as the Federal Bureau of Investigation or the Drug Enforcement Administration.

Long-Term Storage: A location that is designated to secure evidence or property items in the custody of an agency until the items are diverted, sold, released, or destroyed. For the purposes of this handbook, long term storage refers to any location where evidence may be stored for more than 72 hours.

Nonporous Container: Packaging through which liquids or vapors cannot pass (e.g., glass jars, metal cans, and plastic bags) (National Institute of Justice "Crime Scene Investigation: A Guide for Law Enforcement" 2000).

Packaging: Container used to house individual items of evidence.

Parent/Child Tracking: A tracking system capability that maintains information about an original evidence sample (or parent) and the resulting samples (or children) that have been devised or extracted to obtain testing results.

Personal Protective Equipment (PPE): Items used to prevent an individual's direct contact with bloodborne pathogens. PPE includes disposable gloves, disposable overalls, disposable shoe covers, laboratory coats, masks, and eye protection.

Porous Container: Packaging through which liquids or vapors may pass (e.g., paper bags and cloth bags) (National Institute of Justice "Crime Scene Investigation: A Guide for Law Enforcement" 2000).

Property Officer: A worker responsible for the intake, submission, and/or retrieval of evidence in a property room.

Property Room: A location dedicated to housing evidence for criminal investigations. This location can be in a law enforcement office, a crime laboratory, a hospital, or a court.

Property Room Manager/Supervisor: A worker responsible for managing the property and/or the personnel who handles the intake, submission, and/or retrieval of evidence in a property room.

Refrigerated: A storage condition in which the temperature is maintained thermostatically between 2°C and 8°C (36°F and 46°F) with less than 25% humidity.

Refrigerator: Equipment used to keep an item or group of items cooler than room temperature.

Room Temperature: A storage condition in which the temperature is equal to the ambient temperature of its surroundings; storage area may lack temperature and humidity control methods.

Sexual Assault Kit: A collection of items used by medical personnel to collect and preserve physical sexual assault evidence that can be used in a criminal investigation.

Stabilizing Solution: A compound that is added to biological material designed to enable the storage and transportation of DNA samples without freezing (Swinfield et al. 2009).

Standard Operating Procedure (SOP): A set of guidelines that can also be equated to general orders, policies and procedures, and rules and regulations.

Temperature Controlled: A storage condition in which temperature is maintained thermostatically between 15.5°C and 24°C (60°F - 75°F) with less than 60% humidity.

<u>Temporary Storage/Short-Term Storage</u>: Storage of evidence from the time collected to reception by property room personnel. For the purpose of this handbook, temporary or short-term storage refers to any location that can hold evidence for up to 72 hours.

<u>Tickler File</u>: A file that serves as a reminder and is arranged to bring matters to timely attention; can be manual (e.g., folders into which copies of property records are placed when an item is temporarily signed out to the laboratory, court, investigation, etc.), or can be automated as part of a computer application that sets a reminder date that triggers a notification that an action is overdue (e.g., an item has not been returned from court).

<u>Touch DNA</u>: DNA contained in shed skin cells that transfer to surfaces that humans touch (Daly, Murphy, and McDermott 2012).

WORKS CITED

Aggarwal, R. K., J. W. Lang, and L. Singh. 1992. "Isolation of High-Molecular-Weight DNA from Small Samples of Blood Having Nucleated Erythrocytes, Collected, Transported, and Stored at Room Temperature." *Genetic Analysis: Techniques and Applications* 9, no. 2 (April): 54 - 57.

Austin, M. A., J. M. Ordovas, J. H. Eckfeldt, R. Tracy, E. Boerwinkle, J. M. Lalouel, and M. Printz. 1996. "Guidelines of the National Heart, Lung, and Blood Institute Working Group on Blood Drawing, Processing, and Storage for Genetic Studies." *American Journal of Epidemiology* 144, no. 5 (September 1): 437 - 41.

Benecke, Mark. 2004. "Forensic DNA Samples—Collection and Handling." Chap. 103 In *Encyclopedia of Medical Genomics and Proteomics*, edited by Jürgen Fuchs and Maurizio Podda. Dekker Encyclopedias Series, 1420. New York: CRC Press.

Bonnet, Jacques, Marthe Colotte, Delphine Coudy, Vincent Couallier, Joseph Portier, Benedictine Morin, and Sophie Tuffet. 2010. "Chain and Conformation Stability of Solid-State DNA: Implications for Room Temperature Storage." *Nucleic Acids Research* 38, no. 5 (March): 1531 - 46. doi:10.1093/nar/gkp1060.

Caputo, Mariela, Luis A. Bosio, and Daniel Corach. 2011. "Long-Term Room Temperature Preservation of Corpse Soft Tissue: An Approach for Tissue Sample Storage." *Investigative Genetics* 2, no. 17 (August 16): 6. doi:10.1186/2041-2223-2-17.

Centers for Disease Control and Prevention. 2012. "Surface Sampling Procedures for Bacillus Anthracis Spores from Smooth, Non-Porous Surfaces." Last modified April 26, 2012, accessed July 5. http://www.cdc.gov/niosh/topics/emres/surface-sampling-bacillus-anthracis.html.

Daly, Dyan J., Charlotte Murphy, and Sean D. McDermott. 2012. "The Transfer of Touch DNA from Hands to Glass, Fabric and Wood." *Forensic Science International: Genetics* 6, no. 1 (January): 41 - 46. doi:10.1016/j.fsigen.2010.12.016.

Dissing, Jørgen, Annie Søndervang, and Stine Lund. 2010. "Exploring the Limits for the Survival of DNA in Blood Stains." *Journal of Forensic Legal Medicine* 17, no. 7 (October): 392 - 96. doi:10.1016/j.jflm.2010.08.001.

DNA Initiative. 2012. "Glossary." Accessed July 5. http://www.dna.gov/glossary.

Elliott, Paul, and Tim C. Peakman. 2008. "The U.K. Biobank Sample Handling and Storage Protocol for the Collection, Processing and Archiving of Human Blood and Urine." *International Journal of Epidemiology* 37, no. 2 (April): 234 - 44. doi:10.1093/ije/dym276.

Farkas, Daniel H., Karen L. Kaul, Danny L. Wiedbrauk, and Frederick L. Kiechle. 1996. "Specimen Collection and Storage for Diagnostic Molecular Pathology Investigation." *Archives of Pathology and Laboratory Medicine* 120, no. 6: 591 - 96.

Federal Bureau of Investigation. 2013. "Clearances." Accessed April 16. http://www.fbi.gov/about-us/cjis/ucr/crime-in-the-u.s/2011/crime-in-the-u.s.-2011/clearances.

Frippiat, Cristophe, Sabrina Zorbo, Daniel Leonard, Anne Marcotte, Mariella Chaput, Charlotte Aelbrecht, and Fabrice Noel. 2011. "Evaluation of Novel Forensic DNA Storage Methodologies." *Forensic Science International: Genetics* 5, no. 5 (November): 386 - 92. doi:10.1016/j.fsigen.2010.08.007.

Gill, Peter, Alec J. Jeffreys, and David J. Werrett. 1985. "Forensic Application of DNA 'Fingerprints'." *Nature* 318, no. 6046 (December 12): 577 - 79.

Gino, S., C. Robino, and C. Torre. 2000. "DNA Typing of Liquid Blood Samples Stored at 4 Degrees C for 15 Years." In *Progress in Forensic Genetics 8*, edited by George F. Sensabaugh, Patrick J. Lincoln, and Bjørnar Olaisen. Paper presented at the 18th Congress of the International Society for Forensic Genetics, San Francisco, California, August 17 - 21, 1999.

Goray, Mariya, Roland A. H. van Oorschot, and John R. Mitchell. 2012. "DNA Transfer within Forensic Exhibit Packaging: Potential for DNA Loss and Relocation." *Forensic Science International: Genetics* 6, no. 2 (March): 158 - 66. doi:10.1016/j.fsigen.2011.03.013.

Graham, E. A. M., E. E. Turk, and G. N. Rutty. 2008. "Room Temperature DNA Preservation of Soft Tissue for Rapid DNA Extraction: An Addition to the Disaster Victim Identification Investigators Toolkit?". *Forensic Science International: Genetics* 2, no. 1 (January): 29 - 34. doi:10.1016/j.fsigen.2007.07.003.

Greene, Susan, and Miles Moffeit. 2007. "Bad Faith Difficult to Prove." *The Denver Post*, July 22. http://www.denverpost.com/evidence/ci_6429277.

Halsall, Antony, Paul Ravetto, Yancy Reyes, Nicola Thelwell, Alice Davidson, Rupert Gaut, and Stephen Little. 2008. "The Quality of DNA Extracted from Liquid or Dried Blood Is Not Adversely Affected by Storage at 4°C for up to 24 H." *International Journal of Epidemiology* 37, Supplement 1 (April): i7 - i10. doi:10.1093/ije/dym278.

Hampikian, Greg, Emily West, and Olga Akselrod. 2011. "The Genetics of Innocence: Analysis of 194 U.S. DNA Exonerations." *Annual Review of Genomics and Human Genetics* 12 (September): 97 - 120. doi:10.1146/annurev-genom-082509-141715.

HERC (Healthcare Environmental Resource Center). 2012. "Regulated Medical Waste—Overview." Accessed July 5. http://www.hercenter.org/rmw/rmwoverview.cfm.

Kansagara, Anjali G., Heather E. McMahon, and Michael E. Hogan. 2008. "Dry-State, Room-Temperature Storage of DNA and RNA." *Nature Methods* 5, no. 9.

Kanter, E., M. Baird, R. Shaler, and I. Balazs. 1986. "Analysis of Restriction Fragment Length Polymorphisms in Deoxyribonucleic Acid (DNA) Recovered from Dried Bloodstains." *Journal of Forensic Sciences* 31, no. 2: 403 - 08.

Kiley, William P. 2008. "An Impending Crisis: The Property Room Is Full." *The Police Chief* August.

———. 2009. "The Effects of DNA Advances on Police Property Rooms." *The FBI Law Enforcement Bulletin* (March): 20 - 21.

Kilpatrick, C. William. 2002. "Noncryogenic Preservation of Mammalian Tissues for DNA Extraction: An Assessment of Storage Methods." *Biochemical Genetics* 40, no. 1-2 (February): 53 - 62.

Kline, Margaret C., David L. Duewer, Janette W. Redman, John M. Butler, and David A. Boyer. 2002. "Polymerase Chain Reaction Amplification of DNA from Aged Blood Stains: Quantitative Evaluation of the 'Suitability for Purpose' of Four Filter Papers as Archival Media." *Analytical Chemistry* 74, no. 8 (March 15): 1863 - 69. doi:10.1021/ac015715e.

Kobilinsky, L. 1992. "Recovery and Stability of DNA in Samples of Forensic Science Significance." *Forensic Science Review* 4, no. 1: 67 - 87.

Latta, Joseph T., and Gordon A. Bowers. 2011. *Property and Evidence by the Book* Second ed.: International Association for Property and Evidence, Inc.

Lee, Henry C., Elaine M. Pagliaro, Karen M. Berka, Nancy L. Folk, Daniel T. Anderson, Gualberto Ruano, Tim P. Keith, *et al.* 1991. "Genetic Markers in Human Bone: I. Deoxyribonucleic Acid (DNA) Analysis." *Journal of Forensic Sciences* 36, no. 2 (March): 320 - 30.

Lee, Steven B., Kimberly C. Clabaugh, Brie Silva, Kingsley O. Odigie, Michael D. Coble, Odile Loreille, Melissa Scheible, *et al.* 2012. "Assessing a Novel Room Temperature DNA Storage Medium for Forensic Biological Samples." *Forensic Science International: Genetics* 6, no. 1 (January): 31 - 40. doi:10.1016/j.fsigen.2011.01.008.

Lee, Steven B., Cecelia A. Crouse, and Margaret C. Kline. 2010. "Optimizing Storage and Handling of DNA Extracts." *Forensic Science Review* 22, no. 2 (July): 131 - 44.

Lund, Stine, and Jørgen Dissing. 2004. "Surprising Stability of DNA in Stains at Extreme Humidity and Temperature." In *Progress in Forensic Genetics 10*, edited by Ch. Doutremépuich and N. Morling. Paper presented at the 20th Congress of the International Society for Forensic Genetics, Arcachon, France, April 2003.

McCabe, Edward R. B., Shu-Zhen Huang, William K. Seltzer, and Martha L. Law. 1987. "DNA Microextraction from Dried Blood Spots on Filter Paper Blotters: Potential Applications to Newborn Screening." *Human Genetics* 75, no. 3 (March): 213 - 16. doi:10.1007/BF00281061.

Michaud, Corinne L., and David R. Foran. 2011. "Simplified Field Preservation of Tissues for Subsequent DNA Analyses." *Journal of Forensic Sciences* 56, no. 4 (July): 846 - 52. doi:10.1111/j.1556-4029.2011.01771.x.

National Institute of Justice. 2000. "Crime Scene Investigation: A Guide for Law Enforcement." NCJ 178280. Washington, DC: U.S. Department of Justice, Office of Justice Programs, National Institute of Justice, Technical Working Group on Crime Scene Investigation, 58.

———. 2000. "The Future of Forensic DNA Testing: Predictions of the Research and Development Working Group." NCJ 183697. Washington, D.C.: U.S. Department of Justice, Office of Justice Programs, National Institute of Justice, National Commission on the Future of DNA Evidence, Research and Development Working Group, 91.

———. 2002. "Using DNA to Solve Cold Cases." NCJ 194197. Washington, DC: U.S. Department of Justice, Office of Justice Programs, National Institute of Justice, National Commission on the Future of DNA Evidence Crime Scene Investigation Working Group, 32.

National Institute of Justice, and Office of Law Enforcement Standards. 1998. "Forensic Laboratories: Handbook for Facility Planning, Design, Construction, and Moving." NCJ 168106. Washington, D.C.: U.S. Department of Justice, Office of Justice Programs, National Institute of Justice, Technical Working Group, 71.

OSHA (Occupational Safety and Health Administration). 2012. "Bloodborne Pathogens." *Toxic and Hazardous Substances.* 29 CFR 1910.1030, (April 3). http://www.osha.gov/pls/oshaweb/owadisp.show_document?p_table=standards&p_id=10051.

Prinz, M., W. Grellner, and C. Schmitt. 1993. "DNA Typing of Urine Samples Following Several Years of Storage." *International Journal of Legal Medicine* 106, no. 2 (March 1): 75 - 79. doi:10.1007/BF01225044.

Roberts, Katherine A., and Donald J. Johnson. 2012. "Investigations on the Use of Samplematrix to Stabilize Crime Scene Biological Samples for Optimized Analysis and Room Temperature Storage." 237838. Washington D.C.: U.S. Department of Justice, 296.

Ross, K. S., N. E. Haites, and K. F. Kelly. 1990. "Repeated Freezing and Thawing of Peripheral Blood and DNA in Suspension: Effects on DNA Yield and Integrity." *Journal of Medical Genetics* 27, no. 9 (September): 569 - 70.

Seah, L. H., and L. A. Burgoyne. 2001. "Photosensitizer Initiated Attacks on DNA under Dry Conditions and Their Inhibition: A DNA Archiving Issue." *Journal of Photochemistry and Photobiology B: Biology* 61, no. 1-2 (August 15): 10 - 20. doi:10.1016/S1011-1344(01)00132-4.

Sigurdson, A. J., M. Ha, M. Cosentino, T. Franklin, K. A. Haque, Y. Qi, C. Glaser, Y. Reid, and A. W. Bergen. 2006. "Long-Term Storage and Recovery of Buccal Cell DNA from Treated Cards." *Cancer Epidemiology, Biomarkers and Prevention* 15, no. 2 (February): 385 - 88.

Sjöholm, Malin Ida Linnea, Joakim Dillner, and Joyce Carlson. 2007. "Assessing Quality and Functionality of DNA from Fresh and Archival Dried Blood Spots and Recommendations for Quality Control Guidelines." *Clinical Chemistry* 53, no. 8 (August): 1401 - 07. doi:10.1373/clinchem.2007.087510.

Smith, S., and P. A. Morin. 2005. "Optimal Storage Conditions for Highly Dilute DNA Samples: A Role for Trehalose as a Preserving Agent." *Journal of Forensic Sciences* 50, no. 5 (September): 1101 - 08.

Steinberg, Karen K., Karen C. Sanderlin, Chin-Yih Ou, W. Harry Hannon, Geraldine M. McQuillan, and Eric J. Sampson. 1997. "DNA Banking for Epidemiologic Studies." *Epidemiologic Reviews* 19, no. 1 (May): 156 - 62.

Swinfield, Chloe E., Eleanor A. M. Graham, Diane Nuttall, Sabine Maguire, Alison Kemp, and Guy N. Rutty. 2009. "The Use of DNA Stabilizing Solution to Enable Room Temperature Storage and Transportation of Buccal and Trace Sample Swabs." In *Progress in Forensic Genetics 13*, edited by N. Morling. Paper presented at the 23rd Congress of the International Society for Forensic Genetics, Buenos Aires, Argentina, September 2009.

Visvikis, Sophie, Alexandra Schlenck, and Mickaël Maurice. 2005. "DNA Extraction and Stability for Epidemiological Studies." *Clinical Chemistry and Laboratory Medicine* 36, no. 8 (June): 551 - 55. doi:10.1515/CCLM.1998.094.

Wan, Eunice, Matthew Akana, Jennifer Pons, Justin Chen, Stacy Musone, Pui-Yan Kwok, and Wilson Liao. 2010. "Green Technologies for Room Temperature Nucleic Acid Storage." *Current Issues in Molecular Biology* 12: 135 - 42.

Yates, J. R., S. Malcolm, and A. P. Read. 1989. "Guidelines for DNA Banking. Report of the Clinical Genetics Society Working Party on DNA Banking." *Journal of Medical Genetics* 26, no. 4 (April): 245 - 50. doi:10.1136/jmg.26.4.245.

Zhu, Bo, Takao Furuki, Takashi Okuda, and Minoru Sakurai. 2007. "Natural DNA Mixed with Trehalose Persists in B-Form Double-Stranding Even in the Dry State." The *Journal of Physical Chemistry B* 111, no. 20 (May): 5542 - 44. doi:10.1021/jp071974h.

Made in the USA
Monee, IL
05 November 2021